KITCHEN *confidence*

ESSENTIAL RECIPES & TIPS
THAT WILL HELP YOU COOK ANYTHING

KELSEY NIXON

CLARKSON POTTER

NEW YORK

Copyright © 2014 by Kelsey's Kitchen Productions LLC
Photographs copyright © 2014 by Sara Remington

Published in the United States by Clarkson Potter/Publishers, an imprint
of the Crown Publishing Group, a division of Random House LLC, a
Penguin Random House Company, New York.
www.crownpublishing.com
www.clarksonpotter.com

CLARKSON POTTER is a trademark and POTTER with colophon is a
registered trademark of Random House LLC.

COOKING CHANNEL and the COOKING CHANNEL logo are trademarks
of COOKING CHANNEL, LLC, in the United States and/or other countries.
Used under license.

Library of Congress Cataloging-in-Publication Data
Nixon, Kelsey.
   Kitchen confidence/Kelsey Nixon.—First edition.
1. Cooking, American. 2. Kitchens—Management. I. Title.
TX715.N76 2014
   643'.3—dc23   2013014232

ISBN 978-0-7704-3699-5
eBook ISBN 978-0-7704-3700-8

Printed in China

Cover design by Rae Ann Spitzenberger
Cover photography by Sara Remington

10 9 8 7 6 5 4 3 2 1

First Edition

Sweet Pea Soup (page 108)

For my family, especially my mom,
for inspiring a love of food,
and my husband, for always doing the dishes.

Thanks for cheering me on.

Lasagna with Sausage and Butternut Squash (page 136)

CONTENTS

INTRODUCTION

I realize that not everyone feels one hundred percent at home in the kitchen . . . that you may love food—whether that means cooking, eating out, trying a new ingredient, or watching great food being prepared on television—but still might need a helping hand to become a more confident home cook. It doesn't matter if you are just turning on your oven for the first time in a new apartment or looking to up your game when you host the next big family gathering; I'm here to help, your friend in the kitchen to whom you can turn no matter your skill level. *Kitchen Confidence* is within reach.

I grew up in a small town in northern Utah, and my favorite memories are rooted in family dinners or parties with friends where food and cooking were at the center of the celebration. Whether it was the formal Christmas dinner that my mom hosted for our extended family year after year, or a simple summer BBQ on the deck with our neighbors, food was clearly the foundation and catalyst for treasured experiences, conversations, and connections. My upbringing taught me that the process of making a meal and serving it to the people you love is unlike any other; it's a great way to share a little bit of yourself on a plate and show just how much you care.

After a long day at work, my mom would enter the kitchen with a spring in her step and make dinner for our family. She loved it. Thanks to her passion for cooking, I was drawn into the kitchen at a young age and have never looked back. The best conversations I had with my mom growing up happened while she was preparing dinner and I was helping at her side. She made the

kitchen the most comfortable place to be in our home. Starting with family recipes and following her lead, I began to feel comfortable cutting, mixing, and measuring, learning how to make simple dishes like lemon roasted chicken and Sunday pot roast. Spending time with her and the other fantastic cooks in my family, poring over cookbooks on a regular basis, and experimenting a little on my own, I learned essential skills that I knew would serve me for years to come—and I began to relish that unbeatable feeling of making something with my own hands that nourished the people I care about.

My love for food followed me to college, but unfortunately my mom didn't—so no more home-cooked meals every night! It didn't take long for that void to send me straight to my own bite-size dorm kitchen to begin cooking for myself, my roommates, and any prospective boyfriends. In fact, one of the first meals that came out of my college kitchen was a recipe that lives in this book: I served Tortellini with Snap Peas and Lemon-Dill

Cream (page 129) to my now husband the first time I cooked for him.

I was a broadcast journalism student who loved food and television but wasn't all that interested in a news career. So I committed myself to the unorthodox idea of hosting my own cooking show. A lucky break with an internship at *Martha Stewart Living* on the cooking show *Everyday Food* settled things; this was what I wanted to do and I was going to figure out a way to make it happen.

With the wind at my back after such an incredible internship experience, I went back to school my junior year and convinced a supportive professor to let me start a cooking show geared toward college students. I spent the next two years producing and hosting one hundred episodes of *Kelsey's Kitchen* while earning my degree. Culinary school followed soon after. Then, only a few months into my training, I found myself at an audition for *The Next Food Network Star,* where the winner would be granted his or her very own show on Food Network. Great timing paired with lots of hard work and some good luck earned me a spot on the show. Three short weeks after graduating culinary school, I was on a plane headed to New York City to begin filming.

Being on *The Next Food Network Star* was life-changing, exhilarating, and positively frightening—I often refer to the opportunity as the million-dollar experience that I wouldn't pay a dollar to do again. I both won challenges and was at the bottom of the pack my fair share, but ultimately being on the show only solidified my dream. I finished respectably in

fourth place, so I had the privilege of meeting and working with myriad true professionals and gained invaluable experience cooking on camera at a professional level. My college sweetheart and I moved to New York City as newlyweds soon after, and I spent the next couple of years with my head down, working hard, and taking every opportunity that came along. Bobby Flay and others were instrumental in helping me: His production company eventually produced the first season of Cooking Channel's *Kelsey's Essentials* in 2010 and has continued to produce it through its fifth season (and counting).

Whether on the show or at home, I love discussing food. Having the chance to engage and inspire people to cook is something I feel so passionate about. Chatting in the kitchen with friends is one of my favorite ways to spend time. Whether they are beginners or very talented home cooks, it's a blast being inspired by one another, encouraging one another, and discussing our most recent recipe successes and failures. Either way, I love helping with the "whys" behind a recipe's instructions and seeing a friend's confidence soar when we create something so delicious

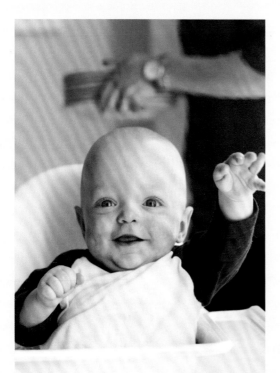

out of our fun time in the kitchen. This book is an extension of my show, conversations with friends, and upbringing in the kitchen.

While my own cooking style and preferences continue to evolve, I find myself consistently returning to the fundamental skills I learned from my mom. I take building-block basics, like lasagna or roasted veggies, and apply a fresh approach for contemporary palates. I'm so excited to share what I think is essential to becoming a great home cook—those must-have tips, tools, and techniques that will allow you to cook with confidence, imagination, and style. With this book, you'll learn the versatility of a well-seasoned cast-iron skillet, the benefits of always having puff pastry dough in your freezer, and the ease of whipping up a quick pan sauce. You'll find secrets for mimicking charcoal-grilled flavors when you are stuck inside, and for making a cake that doesn't require an oven.

In addition to identifying these essentials, this book focuses on the recipes that I believe every home cook should have in her back pocket. From chocolate chip cookies and banana bread to smashed potatoes and pan-seared steaks, these are the dishes that everyone should have a great recipe for—ones that have been elevated and updated for modern-day tastes. My tuna noodle casserole is not the one your mother or grandmother has been making for the last fifty years. (And perhaps that is a good thing!) My favorite buttermilk biscuits are old-fashioned

Tuna Noodle Casserole (page 162)

Once you know some of the hows and whys in the kitchen, and have the recipes to support them, you are well on your way to gaining kitchen confidence and becoming a great home cook, which comes from getting some good old-fashioned practice. Understanding kitchen essentials gives you permission to experiment with recipes—embellishing, adapting, modifying, or even changing them completely to make them your own. When you cook often, you have the freedom to improvise, creating your own signature recipes. Along the way you'll find that you often learn just as much, if not more, from the mistakes, too. Don't let the possibility of mishaps intimidate you from challenging yourself; in our house, if dinner doesn't work out, pizza can always be delivered in twenty minutes. When you approach cooking this way it becomes a creative outlet that allows you to put yourself on a plate. I've included suggestions for variations throughout this book to get you started; they will hopefully spark some great ideas of your own.

I hope that this book will become your well-used kitchen companion, giving you confidence and helping you create joy in the kitchen, and that these dishes will become as trusted as your own family's recipes. Read on, enjoy the creative process, and get cooking!

perfection, though I do share how to jazz them up with bacon, cheddar, and chives. I makeover my mom's classic roast chicken with warm Moroccan spices. Hominy is a surprise ingredient in a spicy vegetarian chili, and picnic-ready slaw gets a distinctive, new flavor with cilantro, lime, and chili garlic sauce. From breakfast to dessert and everything in between, these recipes will provide direction for creating delicious weeknight dinners, potluck treats, party fare, and even holiday meals for you and your loved ones.

ESSENTIAL PANTRY

Having a well-equipped pantry is like having an insurance policy on dinner. Keeping a stockpile of basic pantry essentials ensures that you always have most of the ingredients to make at least a few recipes. If you've got the space and flexibility in your budget, my suggestion is to make a few big trips every year to load up your dry pantry with everything from peanut butter to canned artichoke hearts. Then all you have to do on a weekly basis is fill in the blanks with fresh items like seasonal produce, meats, and fish.

With these staples on hand, you can focus your time more on choosing the fresh ingredients like produce and meats that you'll pick up weekly. Buying each ingredient for a meal as you need it, and having no idea whether you have a duplicate back at home, isn't efficient or cost effective—and before you know it, you'll have four bottles of fish sauce on your pantry shelf! Stocking your pantry shelves with the essentials will also help arm you with the tools you'll need to whip up an impromptu meal when you don't have time to stop at the grocery store. It's the first step to making cooking out of your home kitchen a joy rather than a chore. Here is what I recommend:

FRESH PANTRY

Onions and shallots

Garlic

Potatoes

Lemons

Carrots

Celery

Fresh herbs: My favorites (and the most versatile) are flat-leaf parsley, cilantro, basil, and thyme.

Greek yogurt

Milk

Heavy cream

Eggs

Butter

Cheese: I like having cheddar and Muenster for melting, a soft cheese like mozzarella or goat cheese for salads, Parmesan and feta for finishing dishes, and a few specialty cheeses like Maytag Blue and Brie for assembling a cheese board for a last-minute appetizer. Of course, you don't need to have these all on hand at once!

Good bread

Bacon

Assorted olives

DRY PANTRY AND CONDIMENTS

Extra-virgin olive oil

Vegetable oil

Vinegar: Balsamic, red wine, cider, rice, and sherry vinegar are my favorites.

Wine for cooking (but not what you can buy in the supermarket as "cooking wine")

Chicken and vegetable broth or stock

Low-sodium soy sauce

Worcestershire sauce

Sriracha sauce

Mayonnaise

Ketchup

Whole-grain mustard

Dijon mustard

Jarred salsa verde

Pesto

Honey

Peanut butter

Coconut milk

Canned beans: black, kidney, and white beans especially

Canned tomatoes: whole, diced, and crushed

Tomato paste

Frozen or jarred artichokes

Solid white tuna packed in water

Roasted red peppers

Capers

Pastas and noodles: egg noodles, lasagna, short pasta for quick dinners, vermicelli, etc.

Rice: Jasmine, basmati, and Arborio are all good to have on hand.

Quinoa

Oats

Bread crumbs: plain dry and panko, which are coarser

Cornstarch

Baking powder

Baking soda

Sugar: granulated, brown, and powdered

All-purpose flour

Cornmeal

Cocoa powder (unsweetened)

Chocolate: chocolate chips and other forms of baking chocolate

Dried fruit: raisins, dried currants, dried cranberries

Kosher salt and coarse sea salt

Peppercorns (and a pepper mill of course)

Pure vanilla extract, vanilla beans, or vanilla bean paste

Red pepper flakes

Cayenne pepper

Smoked paprika

Ground coriander

Ground cumin

Herbes de Provence

Ground or whole nutmeg

Ground cinnamon

Dry mustard

Chipotle powder

FREEZER STAPLES

Chicken thighs (my favorite!)

Petite peas

Spinach

Puff pastry dough

Frozen fruit or berries: peaches, mixed berries, bananas

Nuts: pecans, almonds, walnuts

Ice cream (wink!)

organize your kitchen

In order to thrive in your kitchen, it's best to create an organized space that makes cooking easy and accessible. Every couple of months I go through a few simple steps to make sure that my kitchen is in good working order. It's spring cleaning for the kitchen.

DECLUTTER If you haven't used a particular gadget or appliance in a year, get rid of it.

GO VERTICAL Consider putting in pot racks, hooks, and other hanging storage systems to free up counter space.

USE SEE-THROUGH STORAGE If you see it, you're more likely to use it. I love using a modular storage system where the individual containers have pop-top lids that create an airtight seal. I store many of my dried goods like pasta, grains, beans, flour, and sugar in these containers. Things look clean and organized when I open my pantry, and I reach for these items more often because of it.

STORE IT WHERE YOU USE IT Simple rearranging can radically increase your kitchen efficiency. For example, put your wooden spoons in a canister next to the stove rather than in a drawer, and they'll be right there when you need to stir something.

STORE LIKE WITH LIKE Store baking supplies together, creating a nook in your kitchen where things like baking sheets, parchment paper, and mixing bowls can be easily accessed when you're whipping up a batch of cookies or making a layer cake.

REORGANIZE YOUR PANTRY You might find some forgotten items that inspire you, and you can catch and use ingredients before they expire.

ESSENTIAL EQUIPMENT

When it comes to equipment, I believe in quality over quantity. Rather than going to your nearest big box store and buying every single thing on this list at once, I would buy only the absolutely essential things first, investing in the best quality you can afford. (Look for the asterisks to see my top picks that I can't live without.) These pieces will last you for years and you'll be so glad that you made the investment—nice equipment really affects the way your cooking turns out, and in the long run is more economical, as you won't have to replace any of it often. As someone who has lived in very small apartments, with tiny kitchens and zero storage space, I know from experience it's easier to use fewer higher quality items than a kitchen full of equipment that is either on the verge of breaking or rarely necessary, like a corn shucker or an electric can opener. Get the good stuff.

Also, while this list may look long, keep in mind that it's thorough—a list you can grow into. As I just moved into a larger kitchen, I've started to add some "nice to have" and "fun, if you have the room" pieces to my collection, but I survived just fine with the absolutely essential pieces until now!

*THESE ARE THE TOOLS I CONSIDER ESSENTIAL.

COOKWARE

Saucepan with cover
(2- to 3-quart)

Large skillet
(10- to 14-inch)

Small skillet
(7- to 9-inch)

Large nonstick skillet
(10- to 14-inch)

Stockpot (8-quart or larger),
with steamer insert

*Cast-iron skillet (10- to
12-inch; see page 159)

*Dutch oven (6- to 7-quart,
such as Le Creuset; see
page 167)

KNIVES/CUTLERY/UTENSILS

*Paring knife
(3½- to 5-inch; see page 77)

*Chef's knife
(8- to 14-inch; see page 77)

*Serrated knife
(see page 77)

Kitchen shears

Sharpening/honing steel

Large metal spoons
(slotted and solid)

Heatproof/silicone spatula

Wire whisk

*Wooden spoons
(see page 125)

Ladle

*Spring-loaded tongs
(see page 125)

With the right ingredients and equipment, all that's left on the road to kitchen confidence is mastering some key techniques. Since the best way to learn is by doing, I thought it would be most helpful to put these techniques in context, paired with a recipe that puts them to use. Turn to any one of these pages for my top tips to get started or refresh your memory.

BAKING

Dry measuring cup set

Dry measuring spoon set

Liquid measuring cup(s)

Cooling rack(s)

9-inch pie plate

Muffin pan

Loaf pan (9 × 5-inch)

Rimmed baking sheets (9 × 13-inch)

Parchment paper

Rolling pin

Pastry brush

*Bench scraper (see page 208)

Mixing bowls

*Hand mixer (see page 215)

Working with yeast dough (page 41)

Quick-pickling (page 57)

Blanching (page 84)

Pan-roasting (page 123)

Stir-frying (page 128)

Making pan sauces (page 146)

Roasting (page 151)

Indoor grilling (page 157)

Braising (page 167)

Frosting (page 219)

MISCELLANEOUS

*Japanese mandoline (see page 66)

*Wooden cutting board (see page 134)

Sieve (with fine mesh)

Colander

*Zester/grater (such as Microplane; see page 199)

Pepper mill

Vegetable peeler

Can opener

Ice cream scoop

*Blender or food processor (see page 109)

*Digital thermometer (see page 149)

NICE TO HAVE

Roasting pan with rack

Heavy-duty stand mixer

Cast-iron grill pan

9-inch springform pan

Ramekins

FUN, IF YOU HAVE THE ROOM

Potato ricer

Griddle

Rice cooker

Canning equipment

Pizza stone

BREAKFAST & MORNING TREATS

BERRIES AND CREAM CHEESE STUFFED FRENCH TOAST

SERVES **4 to 6** • PREP **20 minutes** • COOK **20 minutes**

1 loaf challah bread, cut into 6 (1½-inch-thick) slices

1 (8-ounce) package cream cheese, at room temperature

¼ cup strawberry jam

½ teaspoon grated lemon zest

½ cup blueberries, plus more for garnish

3 to 5 tablespoons unsalted butter

1 cup whole milk

3 large eggs

1 tablespoon light brown sugar

2 teaspoons vanilla extract

1½ teaspoons ground cinnamon

Powdered sugar, for dusting

Maple syrup, for serving

The only thing better than French toast for breakfast is *stuffed* French toast! And as a bonus, the stuffed version is as simple to make as the classic. I have always loved making this with challah bread: The chewy texture and slightly sweet flavor are perfect, and the structure of the bread allows you to cut big, thick slices, which are easy to stuff. The combination of jam and fresh blueberries mixes wonderfully with the tangy cream cheese, making the filling sweet, tart, and just rich enough. This is one of my go-to recipes for a special occasion breakfast or brunch as it always seems to be a crowd pleaser. If cooking a large batch, transfer the cooked French toast to a baking sheet and keep warm in a 200°F oven while you cook the rest of the slices.

1 Using a sharp paring knife, cut a horizontal slit, 1½ to 2 inches deep, into the bottom crust of each slice of bread to create a pocket for the filling.

2 In a small bowl, beat together the cream cheese, jam, and lemon zest. Fold in the blueberries. Spoon about 2 tablespoons of the mixture into the pocket of each slice of bread.

3 Melt 1 tablespoon of the butter and transfer it to a 9 × 13-inch baking dish. Whisk in the milk, eggs, brown sugar, vanilla, and cinnamon.

4 In a large, heavy skillet set over medium heat, melt 2 tablespoons of the butter.

5 Working in batches (of however many slices you can fit into your skillet at once), put each stuffed slice into the milk mixture, letting each side soak for about 10 seconds. Add the soaked slices to the hot butter in the skillet. Cook until golden brown, 4 to 5 minutes per side, adding more butter to the skillet as needed.

6 Serve warm, topped with extra blueberries, a dusting of powdered sugar, and some maple syrup.

PEANUT BUTTER–STUFFED FRENCH TOAST WITH CARAMELIZED BANANAS Create a peanut butter filling by combining 1 (8-ounce) package softened cream cheese with ¼ cup peanut butter. Follow the technique above for stuffing, soaking, and cooking the French toast. Make the caramelized banana topping by melting 3 tablespoons unsalted butter in a large nonstick skillet over medium-high heat. Add 3 tablespoons dark brown sugar and cook, stirring, until the mixture melts and begins to bubble, about 3 minutes. Cut 2 bananas into ½-inch-thick slices and add to the skillet in a single layer. Cook over medium-high heat, turning once, until warmed through, about 1 minute on each side. Serve the bananas on top of the French toast.

SPICED APPLE–STUFFED FRENCH TOAST Thinly slice 2 gala and 2 McIntosh apples, removing the cores. Melt 1 to 2 tablespoons unsalted butter in a large skillet set over medium-high heat. Add the apples, tossing to coat, and cook until softened, 5 minutes. Sprinkle in 2 tablespoons light brown sugar, 1 tablespoon all-purpose flour, and a pinch each of ground cinnamon, nutmeg, and cloves. Season with kosher salt, remove from the heat, and let cool before using as a stuffing.

BAKED EGGS

WITH SMOKED BACON, SPINACH, AND GOAT CHEESE

The best kind of recipe is one that is so simple, yet fools everyone into thinking that you've been working in the kitchen all morning. These baked eggs are just that sort of dish, and since you can easily adapt it for any number of servings (provided you have enough ramekins), it's a great option for both a cozy breakfast for two, or a brunch for many guests. The smoky and salty flavor of the bacon infuses the eggs and the spinach, which gets sautéed in the drippings. With a hint of tanginess from the mustard, vinegar, and creamy goat cheese and toasted baguette slices to take full advantage of the delicious runny yolk, this recipe will satisfy any breakfast craving.

SERVES 4 • PREP 10 minutes • COOK 30 minutes

6 slices applewood-smoked bacon

6 ounces baby spinach (4 cups loosely packed)

2 teaspoons apple cider vinegar

1 teaspoon whole-grain mustard

Kosher salt and cracked black pepper

4 large eggs

2 ounces goat cheese

Toasted baguette slices, for serving

1 Preheat the oven to 400°F.

2 In a large skillet set over medium heat, cook the bacon until crisp, 8 to 9 minutes. Transfer to a paper towel–lined plate. Once cooled, crumble.

3 Pour off and reserve all but 1 tablespoon of the drippings from the skillet. Add the spinach to the skillet and sauté over medium heat until wilted, 1 to 2 minutes. Stir in the vinegar and mustard, and season to taste with salt and pepper. Continue sautéing until no liquid remains in the skillet, about 2 minutes.

4 Using the reserved drippings, lightly grease 4 (1-cup) ramekins. Carefully crack an egg into each ramekin, being careful not to break the yolks. Season each egg with pepper. Divide the spinach among the ramekins and top with the crumbled bacon.

5 Set the ramekins on a baking sheet. Bake the eggs until the whites are set and the yolks are still runny, 10 to 15 minutes.

6 Top each egg with goat cheese and serve warm with the toasted baguette slices.

PROSCIUTTO, MUSHROOM, AND GRUYÈRE STRATA

SERVES 8 • PREP **25 minutes plus standing time** • COOK **1 hour**

1 loaf French bread, cut or torn into 1-inch cubes (about 8 cups)

2 tablespoons unsalted butter

1 large leek, white and light green parts only, halved lengthwise and sliced crosswise into half-moons (about 1 cup)

10 ounces cremini mushrooms, thinly sliced (about 4 cups)

1 teaspoon kosher salt

2 cups whole milk

1 cup heavy cream

9 large eggs

½ teaspoon cracked black pepper

¼ pound Gruyère cheese, grated (1 cup)

6 ounces prosciutto, diced

2 teaspoons fresh thyme leaves

1 cup shredded Parmesan cheese

A strata is basically a fancy, savory bread pudding, and it can potentially contain everything but the kitchen sink. The ratio of ingredients in this recipe can be used to make all sorts of variations—here I've created a hearty breakfast strata, but you could easily change up the add-ins and serve it as a delicious side dish. Taking the time to toast the bread cubes to dry them out makes a big difference as it contributes to the crispy top, making a great contrast to the rich, custardy center. (If you have a stale loaf of bread lying around, that will do the trick as well, and you can skip the toasting.) For me, the prosciutto, mushrooms, and Gruyère are a match made in heaven: The balance of salty, earthy, and nutty makes this dish so satisfying.

1 Preheat the oven to 350°F. Butter a 9 × 13-inch baking dish.

2 Spread the bread cubes out on a baking sheet. Toast them in the oven until golden brown, stirring once halfway through, about 10 minutes. Remove the bread from the oven to cool, but leave the oven on.

3 Meanwhile, in a large skillet set over medium heat, melt the butter. Add the leek and sauté until softened and beginning to caramelize, 8 to 10 minutes. Add the mushrooms and ½ teaspoon of the salt and cook until the mushrooms are soft, 5 minutes. Remove from the heat and let cool.

4 In a large bowl, whisk together the milk, cream, eggs, pepper, and remaining ½ teaspoon salt.

5 Put the toasted bread cubes, leek and mushroom mixture, Gruyère, prosciutto, and thyme into the prepared baking dish; toss to combine. Pour the milk mixture evenly over the bread mixture. Press down on the bread with a rubber spatula, making sure that it is submerged in the custard. Let stand for at least 10 minutes, allowing the bread to soak up the custard. Top with the Parmesan just before baking.

6 Cover the dish with foil and bake for 20 minutes. Uncover and bake until the center puffs up and sets, 20 to 25 more minutes. Let stand for 5 minutes before serving.

cooking from the hip

When you familiarize yourself with the essentials in the kitchen, an amazing thing happens—you start to develop kitchen confidence. Ultimately, this know-how gives you the ability to improvise in the kitchen. After becoming comfortable with a technique, challenge yourself to swap similar ingredients in and out depending on the season, your mood, your budget, and your time constraints, making your own variations and ultimately creating original recipes. This makes cooking creative and is incredibly fun. The more you practice this approach, the easier it will be to cook from the hip. Being able to open up your refrigerator or pantry and pull a meal together with what you have on hand is a liberating skill that will result in a lot less delivered pizza and a lot more enriching, unique meals for you and your family.

Here are some ideas to get you started:

TRY BRAISING OR DEGLAZING WITH A DIFFERENT LIQUID than what is called for—wine instead of broth, or a combination of juice and water.

USE DIFFERENT ACIDIC ELEMENTS to balance your dish, like lemon or lime juice instead of vinegar.

ADD ALTERNATIVE HERBS, depending on what you have in your fridge. For example, try swapping in fresh dill for chives, or thyme for rosemary.

SWAP OUT VEGETABLES, but keep within the same range of approximate cooking times. For example, hard vegetables like carrots and parsnips can take the place of potatoes and turnips, quicker-cooking vegetables like green beans and asparagus can take the place of snap peas.

QUICHE FLORENTINE

SERVES **8 to 10** • PREP **35 minutes plus chilling time** • COOK **1 hour 5 minutes**

CRUST

1½ cups all-purpose flour, plus more for dusting

½ teaspoon kosher salt

10 tablespoons cold unsalted butter, cut into small cubes

2 tablespoons sour cream

2 to 6 tablespoons ice water

Every good home cook should know how to make a classic quiche, and the one that comes out of my kitchen most often is quiche Florentine. The rich and creamy custard base packed with cheese and spinach cannot be beat—especially with a crust that is as tender and flaky as this one. By keeping the ingredients for the crust really cold and adding a bit of cornstarch to the filling, you're sure to achieve great results. One of the best qualities of quiche is that it is extremely versatile. It can be enjoyed warm right out of the oven or at room temperature, and there is no reason that it cannot be served for breakfast, lunch, or dinner. And the basic method for quiche takes well to substituting ingredients. You could swap out the spinach and Swiss cheese for other veggies, ham or bacon, or cheese that you have in your fridge. Quiche also freezes well after cooking and cooling, making it a great choice for storing and pulling out later for an easy make-ahead meal. To keep the crust flaky, take the quiche out of the freezer the night before and defrost in the refrigerator before reheating in a 400°F oven for 20 minutes. Many times I'll double the recipe and stick one in the freezer to have on hand.

1 **For the crust:** In a food processor, combine the flour and salt and pulse together. Add the cold butter and pulse just until the butter is evenly distributed. Add the sour cream and pulse 2 to 4 more times until just incorporated. Add the ice water 2 tablespoons at a time, pulsing after each addition, just until the dough starts to come together.

2 Turn the dough out onto a piece of plastic wrap and shape it into a disc. Wrap the dough in the plastic wrap and refrigerate for at least 30 minutes.

FILLING

2 tablespoons unsalted butter

2 large leeks (white and light green parts only), chopped

1 (5-ounce) package baby spinach

½ cup heavy cream

½ cup whole milk

4 large eggs

2 teaspoons cornstarch

1 teaspoon kosher salt

¼ teaspoon cracked black pepper

Pinch of cayenne pepper

Pinch of freshly grated nutmeg

¼ pound Swiss cheese, shredded (1 cup)

2 plum tomatoes, seeded and diced

3 Preheat the oven to 375°F.

4 On a floured surface, roll the chilled dough into a 12-inch round that's about ¼ inch thick. Roll the dough up on a rolling pin and gently unroll it into a 9-inch pie pan. Gently press the dough into the pan and trim the overhang to ½ inch. Crimp the edges, and, using a fork, poke holes in the bottom of the crust. Put a piece of parchment paper in the crust and fill it with dried beans or pie weights. Put the pie pan on a large baking sheet and bake until the crust begins to brown around the edges, about 25 minutes. Remove the parchment and dried beans and set the crust aside to cool.

5 **For the filling:** Meanwhile, in a large skillet set over medium heat, melt the butter. Add the leeks and sauté until they soften and begin to caramelize, 8 to 10 minutes. Add the spinach and cook until wilted, about 3 minutes. Remove the pan from the heat and let cool.

6 In a large bowl, whisk together the cream, milk, eggs, cornstarch, salt, black pepper, cayenne, and nutmeg.

7 Scatter the leek and spinach mixture evenly over the bottom of the cooled crust. Top with the Swiss cheese and tomatoes, then pour the milk mixture over the top.

8 Bake until the center is set and the crust is golden brown, 35 to 40 minutes. Let cool on a wire rack.

9 Serve warm or at room temperature. (The quiche will keep wrapped in plastic wrap in the refrigerator for 3 days, or in the freezer for up to 3 months.)

SKILLET SAUSAGE HASH

WITH EGGS

3 tablespoons
extra-virgin olive oil

1 pound sweet Italian
sausage, casings
removed

1 pound baby red
potatoes, quartered

Kosher salt and cracked
black pepper

1 Spanish onion,
chopped

1 red bell pepper,
chopped

1 green bell pepper,
chopped

1 jalapeño, seeded and
minced

2 ounces cheddar
cheese, grated (½ cup)

4 large eggs

When I was growing up, my dad didn't cook much, but when he did, I was always surprised by his skills. On the weekends, I remember him making fantastic breakfast potatoes and delicious hash.

Making a good breakfast hash is practically foolproof. It is an excellent way to use up lonely vegetables in the refrigerator and it's flexible enough that you almost always have the ingredients to make it—as long as you have at least one starchy vegetable, like potatoes. But the final thing that makes this recipe a real winner, especially for my dad, is the fact that you'll need to wash only one pan, which I doubt is a coincidence, as he is also the designated dishwasher in the family.

SERVES **4** · PREP **15 minutes** · COOK **35 minutes**

1 In a large heavy skillet set over medium-high heat, heat 1 tablespoon of the oil. Add the sausage and cook, breaking it up with a wooden spoon, until browned, about 5 minutes. Transfer it to a paper towel–lined plate.

2 Add the remaining 2 tablespoons oil to the same skillet and heat over medium-high heat. Add the potatoes, season liberally with salt and black pepper, and sauté until golden brown, 10 to 12 minutes. Add the onion, bell peppers, and jalapeño, and cook for 5 minutes. Stir in the cooked sausage and cheddar, and season to taste with salt and black pepper.

3 Crack the eggs onto the hash in the skillet. Cover with a lid and cook until the eggs are set, 8 to 10 minutes. Divide the hash and eggs among 4 plates and serve.

ESSENTIAL CRÊPES WITH VARIATIONS

SERVES **12** (MAKES **24**) • PREP **10 minutes plus standing time** • COOK **20 minutes**

2½ cups whole milk

5 large eggs

⅓ cup (⅔ stick) unsalted butter, melted and cooled

1 cup all-purpose flour

2 tablespoons sugar

1 teaspoon kosher salt

Learning how to make crêpes is like earning an important merit badge: Everyone should have this recipe in his or her cooking repertoire. Once you know the simple ratio of ingredients and special method for cooking them, crêpes become a foolproof foundation for a variety of dishes. I first began making crêpes in college when my roommates and I bought into the sweeping trend of campus dessert parties—we'd have so much fun making a big batch of crêpes and setting out a variety of fillings and toppings. Served simply with berries, ricotta, and honey, or apples, cheddar cheese, and walnuts, they make a delicious breakfast, lunch, or dessert.

1 In a blender, combine the milk, eggs, butter, flour, sugar, and salt and blend until smooth. Refrigerate the batter for 1 hour.

2 When you're ready to make the crêpes, blend the mixture once more.

3 Heat a small (10-inch) nonstick skillet over medium-high heat. Using a ¼-cup measuring cup, pour ¼ cup of the batter into the skillet and immediately tilt the skillet so that the batter coats the entire bottom of the pan. Cook until the crêpe starts to bubble on top and is golden brown on the bottom, about 1 minute. Flip the crêpe and cook for 30 more seconds. Transfer to a plate and repeat the process with the remaining batter.

FRESH HERB CRÊPES WITH GOAT CHEESE FILLING AND TOASTED WALNUTS Add ¼ cup finely chopped herbs (tarragon, parsley, chervil, chives, or a mixture) to the batter before cooking. For the filling, mix ¾ pound goat cheese, ½ cup Greek yogurt, and ½ cup cottage cheese in a food processor or blender until smooth. Season to taste with kosher salt and cracked black pepper. Fold in ¼ cup finely chopped toasted walnuts (see page 203). Spread 2 to 3 tablespoons of the filling evenly over each warm crêpe. Fold into quarters and serve.

LAYERED CRÊPE CAKE Try layering 24 prepared crêpes with a sweet filling like lemon cream. Whip 1½ cups heavy cream and ¼ cup powdered sugar until soft peaks form. Working in thirds, with a rubber spatula, fold in ¾ cup store-bought lemon curd until fully combined. Layer the crêpes on a platter or cake plate with 3 tablespoons of the filling evenly spread between each layer. Use the remaining lemon cream to spread over the top. Refrigerate until set, about 2 hours. Cut into wedges and served with crumbled shortbread cookies on top, if desired.

BANANA BREAD

½ cup (1 stick) plus
3 tablespoons unsalted
butter, at room
temperature, plus more
for the pan

1 cup sugar

2 large eggs, at room
temperature

3 large ripe bananas,
mashed

1 teaspoon vanilla extract

2 cups all-purpose flour

1 teaspoon baking soda

¼ teaspoon kosher salt

When bananas on my countertop start to develop dark freckles, I can't help myself from thinking exclusively about banana bread every time I enter the kitchen. This super-soft and moist quick bread manages to feature fresh banana flavor front and center while also allowing the vanilla and butter, which I also like to brush over the baked loaf, to really shine. This recipe is also a great option when you need an easy food gift for a friend or neighbor: Showing up on someone's doorstep with a warm loaf of banana bread will make anyone's day.

MAKES **one 9 × 5-inch loaf** · PREP **15 minutes** · COOK **1 hour**

1 Preheat the oven to 350°F. Butter a 9 × 5 × 3-inch loaf pan and dust with flour.

2 In the bowl of a stand mixer fitted with the paddle attachment, beat together ½ cup of the butter and the sugar until light and fluffy. Beat in the eggs, one at a time, beating well after each addition. Beat in the bananas, vanilla, and 2 tablespoons water.

3 In a large bowl, whisk together the flour, baking soda, and salt. Slowly add the flour mixture to the banana mixture and mix just to combine; be careful not to overmix.

4 Pour the batter into the prepared loaf pan. Bake until golden brown and a cake tester inserted into the center of the loaf comes out clean, about 1 hour. Remove the pan from the oven and let cool for 10 minutes.

5 Melt the remaining 3 tablespoons butter. Carefully remove the loaf from the pan. Brush the top and sides with the melted butter, wrap in foil, and let cool completely. (Store at room temperature for up to 2 days.)

GREEN SMOOTHIE

SERVES 4 • PREP 10 minutes

2 cups baby spinach

1½ cups green grapes, frozen

1 cup cubed fresh pineapple

2 kiwifruits, peeled and quartered

1 Granny Smith apple, cored and quartered

1 banana

2 cups crushed ice

I've always been a fan of a smoothie for breakfast. It's quick, easy, and can be packed with all sorts of healthy ingredients to give your body a boost in the morning. Green smoothies are especially full of nutrients, vibrant in both color and taste, and the perfect way to check off a few of your daily servings of fruits and vegetables. You can pat yourself on the back for getting a serving of spinach or kale in before 8 a.m. Plus they really do taste delicious—trust me! My favorite ingredients in this particular smoothie are the frozen green grapes, which give it great texture, and the kiwi, which adds a little unexpected acidity.

Put the spinach, grapes, pineapple, kiwi, apple, banana, and ice in a blender. Blend until smooth.

ESSENTIAL BUTTERMILK
BISCUITS

WITH VARIATIONS

MAKES 12 biscuits • PREP 15 minutes • COOK 20 minutes

This is one of my go-to recipes when it comes to showers of any kind. Whether celebrating a new baby or bride-to-be, the showers I throw usually occur in the late morning or early afternoon. These tender biscuits are great on their own, and, with just a couple of additional ingredients, they can easily swing from super savory to sweet.

3 cups all-purpose flour

3 tablespoons sugar

4 teaspoons baking powder

1½ teaspoons kosher salt

1 teaspoon baking soda

¾ cup (1½ sticks) cold unsalted butter, cut into small pieces or grated

1 cup buttermilk

1 Preheat the oven to 425°F. Line a baking sheet with parchment paper.

2 In a large bowl, whisk together the flour, sugar, baking powder, salt, and baking soda.

3 Using a pastry cutter or your fingertips, cut the cold butter into the dry ingredients until the mixture resembles a coarse meal. Be careful not to overwork—you really want to see those bits of butter scattered throughout the dough. Add the buttermilk and stir just until moistened.

4 For each biscuit, scoop out about ⅓ cup of the dough and drop it onto the prepared baking sheet, spacing the biscuits about 2 inches apart. Bake until the biscuits are golden brown on top and a tester inserted into the center of one comes out clean, 15 to 20 minutes.

5 Serve warm.

BACON, CHEDDAR, AND CHIVE BISCUITS After cutting in the butter, add 7 slices of cooked and chopped bacon, 1½ cups shredded cheddar cheese, and ¼ cup chopped fresh chives to the dough. Bake as directed above and serve warm with melted butter or good-quality fig jam.

ALMOND
SCONES

This scone recipe has become famous in the neighborhood where I grew up. It's been passed from neighbor to neighbor and seems to pop up at every local function, from baby showers to birthday parties. These tender scones have a rich flavor and a cakey texture, and are easy to make since all of the ingredients come straight from the pantry. I often make a double batch and freeze the extra uncooked triangles in zip-top plastic bags so that I can bake them as needed—just remove the scones from the freezer while the oven is preheating, no additional thawing necessary.

SCONES

2½ cups all-purpose flour

⅓ cup sugar

1 tablespoon baking powder

½ cup (1 stick) plus 3 tablespoons cold unsalted butter, cut into small pieces

1 cup cold heavy cream, plus more if needed

ALMOND ICING

1 cup powdered sugar

¼ teaspoon almond extract

1½ tablespoons whole milk

½ cup sliced almonds, toasted (see page 203)

1 **For the scones:** Preheat the oven to 375°F. Line a baking sheet with parchment paper.

2 In a large bowl, whisk together the flour, sugar, and baking powder. Using a pastry blender, 2 forks, or your hands, cut in the butter until the mixture resembles a coarse meal. Add the 1 cup cream and stir just until the dough comes together. Add more cream, 1 tablespoon at a time, if the dough is too dry.

3 Turn out onto a lightly floured surface and knead gently until a smooth dough is formed. (Do not overwork or the dough will be tough.) Shape into a square about 1 inch thick. Cut the dough into 4 squares, and then cut each square into fourths diagonally for a total of 16 triangles. Transfer the triangles to the prepared baking sheet.

4 Bake until golden brown, 15 to 20 minutes. Transfer the scones to a wire rack and let cool slightly before icing.

5 **For the icing:** In a small bowl, whisk together the powdered sugar and almond extract. Add the milk, a little at a time, until the icing is loose enough to drizzle.

6 Dip the end of the whisk into the icing and wave it over the warm scones to drizzle. Top each iced scone with sliced almonds. (The scones will keep in an airtight container at room temperature for 2 days.)

BLUEBERRY MUFFINS

MAKES **1 dozen** • PREP **10 minutes** • COOK **30 minutes**

3 cups plus 1 tablespoon all-purpose flour

4 teaspoons baking powder

¼ teaspoon baking soda

1 teaspoon kosher salt

1 cup sugar

1 cup sour cream

½ cup (1 stick) unsalted butter, melted

½ cup buttermilk

2 large eggs

½ pint fresh blueberries (heaping 1 cup)

My husband loves blueberry muffins—they were by far his most requested recipe during our first year of marriage. But I was shocked when he started asking for them at dinnertime. Turns out that when he was growing up, it was a tradition in his family to have blueberry muffins with dinner. I have since warmed to the idea, embracing a quirky family tradition. While I still prefer making these on a lazy weekend morning, these muffins, with their tender, delicate crumb and tangy blueberries scattered throughout, are satisfying just about any time—even dinner. Warmed with butter, I'll enjoy one for dessert, and the leftovers are perfect for breakfast the next morning!

1 Preheat the oven to 350°F. Line a standard muffin tin with paper liners.

2 In a large bowl, whisk together 3 cups of the flour, the baking powder, baking soda, and salt.

3 In a separate large bowl, whisk together the sugar, sour cream, melted butter, buttermilk, and eggs.

4 Add the dry ingredients to the wet ingredients and mix until just combined; do not overmix. Toss the blueberries with the remaining 1 tablespoon flour, shake off the excess, and fold them into the batter. Divide the batter evenly among the muffin cups.

5 Bake until a cake tester inserted into a muffin comes out clean, 25 to 30 minutes. Cool slightly in the pan before transferring to a wire rack; serve warm. (The muffins will keep in an airtight container at room temperature for 2 to 3 days.)

LEMON-GLAZED BLUEBERRY MUFFINS Add 1 teaspoon grated lemon zest to the dry ingredients. Make a glaze by whisking together $1/3$ cup powdered sugar, $2\frac{1}{2}$ tablespoons lemon juice, and $1/8$ teaspoon grated lemon zest, adding more lemon juice or powdered sugar as needed until the consistency is perfect for drizzling. Let the muffins cool slightly, then drizzle the glaze over them. Serve warm.

ORANGE-RASPBERRY MUFFINS Add 1 teaspoon grated orange zest to the dry ingredients and replace the blueberries with raspberries.

BLACKBERRY-ALMOND MUFFINS Add $1/2$ teaspoon almond extract to the wet ingredients and replace the blueberries with blackberries.

CINNAMON BUNS

WITH CREAM CHEESE GLAZE

My first experience tackling cinnamon buns was in college. I remember the intense feeling of satisfaction as I pulled my first batch out of the oven, the aroma of fresh bread and spices filling the apartment. This recipe has been years in the making as I've searched for that perfect cinnamon roll, one that has a soft gooey center and plenty of cinnamon flavor but that isn't too sweet. I can't get enough of how the tang in the cream cheese glaze tempers the decadence of these big rolls. Every family needs a cinnamon bun recipe that they rely on for special weekend breakfasts, and this one is definitely the go-to in my house. You can even assemble these the night before and let them rise in the refrigerator overnight—then all you have to do in the morning is bake them!

MAKES 1 dozen • PREP **20 minutes plus rising time** • COOK **20 minutes**

DOUGH

2 (.25-ounce) packets active dry yeast (4½ teaspoons)

2 cups warm whole milk (105° to 110°F)

5 to 6 cups all-purpose flour

⅓ cup sugar

⅓ cup unsalted butter, melted

1 large egg

2 teaspoons kosher salt

FILLING

⅓ cup packed light brown sugar

1 tablespoon ground cinnamon

½ cup (1 stick) unsalted butter, at room temperature

1 **For the dough:** In the bowl of a stand mixer fitted with the paddle attachment, combine the yeast and warm milk; let stand for 5 minutes until bubbly. Turn the mixer on low and add 1½ cups of the flour, the sugar, melted butter, egg, and salt. Increase the speed to medium and mix for 2 minutes. One cup at a time, add an additional 3½ cups flour and mix until the flour is fully incorporated and the dough pulls away from the sides of the bowl. Add more flour if the dough is too sticky or not pulling away from the sides of the bowl. The dough should be soft, not stiff. Transfer the dough to a large greased bowl, cover with a clean kitchen towel or plastic wrap, and let rise in a warm place until doubled in size, about 1 hour.

2 Punch the dough down and turn it out onto a well-floured surface. Using a lightly floured rolling pin, roll the dough out into a 12 × 8-inch rectangle.

continued

CREAM CHEESE GLAZE

1 cup powdered sugar

1 (4-ounce) package
cream cheese, at room
temperature

¼ cup (½ stick)
unsalted butter, at room
temperature

¼ cup whole milk

1 teaspoon vanilla extract

3 **For the filling:** In a small bowl, combine the brown sugar and cinnamon. Spread the softened butter evenly over the dough, then sprinkle with the cinnamon-sugar mixture.

4 Starting with a long side, roll up the dough tightly. Trim the ends and cut the roll into twelve 1-inch-thick slices. Place the rolls, cut side down, in a greased 9 × 13-inch baking dish and cover with a kitchen towel. Let rise in a warm place until doubled in size, 20 to 30 minutes. (You can also prep the rolls to this stage the night before and let them rise in the refrigerator overnight; just bring the rolls to room temperature the next morning before proceeding.)

5 Preheat the oven to 375°F.

6 Bake the rolls until the tops are light golden brown, 15 to 20 minutes. Let cool in the pan.

7 **For the glaze:** Meanwhile, using a hand or stand mixer, beat together the powdered sugar, cream cheese, butter, milk, and vanilla until smooth.

8 Drizzle the glaze over the cooled rolls. (The cinnamon rolls can be stored in an airtight container at room temperature for 2 to 3 days.)

SWEET ORANGE ROLLS Substitute a filling of ½ cup sugar and the zest and juice of 1 orange for the cinnamon sugar. Substitute a glaze of 1 cup powdered sugar, 2 to 4 tablespoons orange juice, 1 teaspoon grated orange zest, and 4 tablespoons softened unsalted butter for the cream cheese glaze.

WORKING WITH YEAST DOUGH

Nothing smells quite as good as a yeast dough rising and then baking in the oven. Working with yeast doughs (see pages 39, 63, and 168 for recipes) is really easy and super satisfying.

Keep these tips in mind and you'll have great success:

ALWAYS PROOF THE ACTIVE DRY YEAST by dissolving it in lukewarm water (105° to 115°F) and adding a pinch of sugar. Sugar feeds the yeast, helping it bloom. Five to ten minutes later, the yeast should be activated, looking creamy and bubbly, and is now ready to use. If your yeast doesn't bubble, it is dead—and therefore won't make your bread rise— so toss it out and try again with a new packet.

Once you've mixed your dough, DEVELOP THE GLUTEN BY KNEADING. Gluten is a protein whose strands will become elastic after being worked with your hands. The elasticity will help give the dough a great chewy texture. When kneading, focus on using the heel of your palm to push the dough and really work it—don't be too gentle. This is my favorite part—it's a very tactile process and I like the feel of manipulating the dough.

After kneading, SET THE DOUGH ASIDE TO REST AND RISE. Many recipes will instruct you to wait until it's doubled in size. To assist with this, place the dough in a greased bowl, cover it with a clean kitchen towel, and put it in the warmest part of the kitchen.

When you are ready to bake, HAVE SOME FUN WITH SHAPING THE DOUGH. My go-to method for making dinner rolls is to form the dough into a ball, then roll the dough in a quick circular motion in the palm of my hand until a small knot is formed on the bottom. Then I place each roll knot side down for baking. For something less traditional, consider tying your dough into knots or braiding it. You can also stick smaller balls together in a loaf pan to simulate pull-apart bread. Snipping the tops of your rolls or loaves with scissors or slashing with a sharp knife adds a decorative element.

STARTERS

TOMATILLO GUACAMOLE 44

HOT ARTICHOKE DIP WITH ROASTED RED PEPPERS AND KALE 45

ANTIPASTI BRUSCHETTA 46

GRILLED SHRIMP RÉMOULADE COCKTAIL 48

GREEN GODDESS DIP 49

DEVILED EGGS WITH CANDIED BACON 50

CRAB CAKE CROQUETTES WITH HOMEMADE TARTAR SAUCE 52

FRIED HOMEMADE PICKLES WITH RANCH DRESSING 55

FENNEL AND SAUSAGE STUFFED MUSHROOMS 58

GLAZED BUFFALO CHICKEN WINGS WITH BUTTERMILK-BLUE CHEESE DRESSING 60

GRILLED FLATBREAD 63

CARAMELIZED ONION-TOMATO JAM 67

RATATOUILLE TART 69

TOMATILLO GUACAMOLE

SERVES **4 to 6** • PREP **10 minutes**

8 tomatillos, husked, rinsed, and coarsely chopped

¾ cup coarsely chopped fresh cilantro leaves

1 avocado, diced

½ onion, coarsely chopped

½ jalapeño, coarsely chopped (with seeds)

2 garlic cloves, smashed

Juice of 1 lime

1 teaspoon ground cumin

1 teaspoon kosher salt

Tortilla chips, for serving

My husband, Robby, is one of my best taste testers—and a tough critic! He spent a few years living in Mexico and became enamored of the food. I've been on a mission ever since to try and impress the authentic palate that he developed while there. While he's not always convinced by every experiment, he became an instant fan of this fresh, tart take on guacamole. The secret is in the raw tomatillos, and I'd be lying if I didn't admit that adding them uncooked was his idea. He is my better half for more reasons than one.

In a food processor or blender, combine the tomatillos, cilantro, avocado, onion, jalapeño, garlic, lime juice, cumin, and salt and pulse until combined. Serve with tortilla chips.

ROASTED TOMATILLO GUACAMOLE For a deeper flavor and texture, try roasting the tomatillos whole. Preheat the oven to low broil. Place the tomatillos on a baking sheet and put it on the highest oven rack. Broil until the tomatillos have softened and are slightly charred, 7 to 10 minutes. Remove the pan from the oven and let cool for 5 minutes. Add the tomatillos to the food processor along with the other ingredients in the main recipe.

HOT ARTICHOKE DIP
WITH ROASTED RED PEPPERS AND KALE

SERVES **8** • PREP **20 minutes** • COOK **40 minutes**

Throwing together a dip is a must for me any time we have people over. It's easy, satisfying, and buys me some extra time in the kitchen while our guests nosh. This hot dip is super creamy and equally delicious when served with crispy chips or toasted baguette slices. The roasted red pepper adds a great pop of color. If you want to add a bit of a spicy kick, consider adding a chopped poblano or minced jalapeño as well. You could also substitute a 10-ounce package of frozen baby spinach (thawed and squeezed dry) for the kale, making more of a traditional spinach-artichoke dip like the one that we all know and love.

1 bunch kale, stems removed, leaves roughly chopped (about 2 cups)

2 (14-ounce) cans artichoke hearts, drained and chopped

$\frac{1}{3}$ cup roasted red peppers, chopped

4 ounces cream cheese, at room temperature

$\frac{1}{2}$ cup mayonnaise

$\frac{1}{4}$ cup sour cream

2 garlic cloves, minced

$1\frac{1}{3}$ cups grated Parmesan cheese

$\frac{1}{4}$ pound white cheddar cheese, shredded (1 cup)

Toasted baguette slices, for serving

1 Preheat the oven to 375°F.

2 In a medium saucepan, bring salted water to a boil. Add the kale and boil until tender, about 5 minutes. Drain, rinse under cold water, and squeeze out any excess water. Transfer to a cutting board or food processor and finely chop.

3 In a large bowl, stir together the kale, artichokes, roasted red peppers, cream cheese, mayonnaise, sour cream, garlic, and 1 cup of the Parmesan. Spread the mixture evenly in a shallow 1-quart baking dish. Top with the cheddar and remaining $\frac{1}{3}$ cup Parmesan.

4 Bake until bubbling and browned in spots, 25 to 30 minutes. Serve warm with the toasted baguette slices.

ANTIPASTI BRUSCHETTA

1 pint grape tomatoes, quartered

2½ cups mixed olives, pitted and chopped

1 (14-ounce) can water-packed artichoke hearts, drained and chopped

4 pickled pepperoncini peppers, sliced

1 tablespoon brine from the pickled pepperoncini

8 ounces fresh mozzarella cheese, diced

1 garlic clove, minced

Grated zest of ½ lemon

2 tablespoons fresh lemon juice

½ cup extra-virgin olive oil, plus more for brushing

2 tablespoons truffle oil (optional), plus more for drizzling

1 baguette, cut on an angle into ½-inch-thick slices

12 slices prosciutto, halved crosswise

6 fresh basil leaves, chopped

This recipe combines two of the best ways to start just about any meal—antipasti and bruschetta. Here, I've repackaged an antipasto platter into something that is easy to eat, excellent to make ahead, colorful, and great for entertaining. Those classic, favorite antipasto ingredients—salty olives, juicy tomatoes, spicy pepperoncini, creamy mozzarella, bright lemon zest, and more—form a tangy chopped salad that sits atop perfectly crisp bread. The salad actually improves when prepared in advance since the extra time lets the flavors develop. For a lighter take on this dish, try spooning the antipasti salad into small Bibb lettuce cups and serving them the way you would serve lettuce wraps.

SERVES 8 · PREP 20 minutes plus standing time · COOK 10 minutes

1 In a large bowl, combine the tomatoes, olives, artichoke hearts, pepperoncini peppers and brine, mozzarella, garlic, lemon zest, lemon juice, olive oil, and 2 table-spoons truffle oil (if using). Toss and set aside to allow the flavors to marry, about 1 hour.

2 Preheat a grill or grill pan to medium-high.

3 Brush both sides of each baguette slice with olive oil. Grill the baguette slices, turning them once, until crispy and grill marks appear, about 3 minutes per side. Transfer to a serving platter.

4 Top each piece of grilled bread with ½ slice prosciutto and 1 heaping tablespoon of the tomato mixture. Drizzle with more truffle oil, if desired, and sprinkle with the basil.

DEVILED
EGGS

WITH CANDIED BACON

A very happy consequence of developing this recipe was the discovery of candied bacon and just how easy it is to make! This recipe is a great example of how one new ingredient can transform a classic: The bacon's sweet heat and salty, smoky punch make these eggs "devilish" in a whole new way.

SERVES **6 to 8** · PREP **25 minutes** · COOK **20 minutes**

1½ tablespoons light brown sugar

¼ teaspoon plus a pinch of cayenne pepper

Pinch of ground cinnamon

3 slices thick-cut bacon

8 large eggs, cold

⅓ cup mayonnaise

2 teaspoons whole-grain mustard

1 tablespoon apple cider vinegar

1 teaspoon Worcestershire sauce

2 scallions, minced

1 tablespoon finely chopped fresh dill, plus more for garnish

½ teaspoon kosher salt

Sweet paprika, for garnish

1 Preheat the oven to 350°F.

2 In a small bowl, combine the brown sugar, a pinch of the cayenne, and the cinnamon. Put the bacon on a wire rack set over a rimmed baking sheet and sprinkle with some of the spiced sugar.

3 Bake for 10 minutes. Flip the bacon, sprinkle with the remaining spiced sugar, and bake until crispy, about 10 minutes more. Once cool, chop the bacon.

4 Meanwhile, put the cold eggs in a medium saucepan and cover with cold water. Bring to a boil over high heat, remove the pan from the heat, and cover. Let stand for 12 minutes. Drain the eggs and rinse with cold water. Let the eggs cool for 3 minutes and then peel them while they are still warm.

5 In a medium bowl, combine the mayonnaise, mustard, vinegar, Worcestershire sauce, scallions, dill, salt, remaining ¼ teaspoon cayenne, and three-fourths of the chopped bacon.

6 Halve the eggs lengthwise. Gently remove the yolks by pressing your thumb against the back of the yolk to pop it out of the white. Add the yolks to the bowl of mayonnaise mixture. Using a fork, mash together until smooth.

7 Using a tablespoon, carefully spoon the filling into the egg whites. Sprinkle with the paprika, the remaining chopped bacon, and dill before serving.

CRAB CAKE CROQUETTES

WITH HOMEMADE TARTAR SAUCE

SERVES **8 to 10** • PREP **25 minutes** • COOK **45 minutes**

This is my go-to crab cake recipe, which I developed for a Maryland lump crabmeat cook-off. It was a friendly competition with colleagues, but my competitive spirit got the better of me and I really got into it, spending an entire week making different versions for my husband, Robby, in our tiny shoebox kitchen. With each passing day, his despair at eating crab cakes again increased. I'm certain that I spent our entire grocery budget that week on crabmeat alone. Along the way, I achieved a nice balance of tanginess and heat and discovered the trick to the perfect texture—tender on the inside and crispy on the outside—by making them into these bite-size croquettes. In the end, these were delicious enough to not only be embraced by Robby, even on Day 7, but also to score a sweet win at the cook-off.

TARTAR SAUCE

½ cup mayonnaise

2 tablespoons whole-grain mustard

1 tablespoon chili garlic sauce or Sriracha sauce

1 tablespoon fresh lemon juice

2 tablespoons finely chopped cornichons

1 tablespoon finely chopped fresh flat-leaf parsley

Kosher salt and cracked black pepper

CROQUETTES

2 tablespoons vegetable oil, plus more for frying

½ red bell pepper, finely chopped

1 rib celery, finely chopped

1 **For the tartar sauce:** In a small bowl, combine the mayonnaise, mustard, chili garlic sauce, lemon juice, cornichons, and parsley. Season to taste with salt and pepper. Cover and refrigerate until ready to use. (The sauce will keep in an airtight container in the refrigerator for up to 3 days.)

2 **For the croquettes:** In a straight-sided, 10-inch, heavy sauté pan set over medium-high heat, heat the 2 tablespoons oil. Add the bell pepper, celery, onion, and jalapeño and cook, stirring, until softened, about 5 minutes. Transfer to a large bowl and let cool for about 10 minutes. Wipe out the skillet and set aside.

½ small red onion, finely chopped

½ jalapeño, finely chopped (with or without seeds)

1 pound lump crabmeat, coarsely chopped

3 cups plain dry bread crumbs

½ cup mayonnaise

2 teaspoons chili garlic sauce

1 tablespoon fresh lemon juice

1 large egg, beaten

Kosher salt and cracked black pepper

3 To the cooled vegetables, add the crabmeat, 1½ cups of the bread crumbs, the mayonnaise, chili garlic sauce, lemon juice, and egg. Season with salt and pepper and stir well. Put the remaining 1½ cups bread crumbs in a shallow bowl.

4 Shape the crab mixture (about 1½ tablespoons) into bite-size croquettes (2-inch balls, cylinders, or discs), making 25 to 30 total. Coat each piece in the bread crumbs, and arrange them on a parchment paper–lined baking sheet. Cover and refrigerate for at least 1 hour and up to 8 hours.

5 In the same heavy skillet set over medium-high heat, heat ¼ inch of vegetable oil. Working in batches, add the croquettes and cook, turning once, until golden brown and cooked through, 2 to 3 minutes total. Transfer to a paper towel–lined plate and season with salt.

6 Arrange the croquettes on a serving platter with tartar sauce for dipping, and serve hot.

CRAB CAKE SLIDERS Another way to serve these crab cakes that is also great for parties is to make them into sliders. Shape the crab cake mixture into small patties (about ⅓ cup each), making 12 cakes in total. Shallow-fry as directed above, increasing the cooking time to 6 to 8 minutes total. Serve the sliders on toasted and buttered rolls that are about 3 inches in diameter, smeared with the homemade tartar sauce and topped with celery leaves.

FRIED HOMEMADE PICKLES

WITH RANCH DRESSING

SERVES **6 to 8** • PREP **20 minutes plus standing time** • COOK **35 minutes**

Pickles were not just a pregnancy craving for me; they have been a lifelong one! My favorite pickles come from a restaurant in New York City called Ed's Lobster Bar. They are made in-house and top the restaurant's famous lobster rolls. I always order an extra side of these pickles and usually end up leaving with a pint of them to keep in my refrigerator as well. My homemade quick pickles are ready to go in just about 20 minutes, and channel the original. You can eat them as is, of course, stopping after step 3, or carry on with the recipe and do as they do in the South and fry them! Served as an appetizer before dinner, these little pickle chips, with creamy, dill-infused ranch dressing for dipping, are addictive, fun, and a definite conversation starter.

QUICK PICKLES

2 cups red wine vinegar

1½ cups sugar

¼ cup kosher salt

1 teaspoon mustard seeds

¾ teaspoon coriander seeds

½ teaspoon celery seeds

¼ teaspoon whole black peppercorns

2 garlic cloves, smashed

1 red Fresno chile, halved lengthwise

6 Kirby cucumbers (about 2 pounds)

1 **For the pickles:** In a large saucepan set over medium-high heat, combine the vinegar, sugar, salt, mustard seeds, coriander seeds, celery seeds, peppercorns, garlic, chile, and 2 cups water. Bring the mixture to a boil, stirring to dissolve the sugar and salt.

2 Meanwhile, using a mandoline (or sharp knife), cut the cucumbers crosswise into ¼-inch-thick slices and put them in a large heatproof bowl or container.

3 Once the vinegar mixture is boiling, pour it over the sliced cucumbers, making sure the cucumbers are submerged. Let sit in the liquid for about 20 minutes. (The longer the pickles sit in the liquid, the softer they become; for me, 20 minutes is perfect.) Drain the pickles. You can eat these right away or transfer to an airtight container and refrigerate for up to 1 week.

continued

RANCH DRESSING

½ cup buttermilk

½ cup mayonnaise

2 tablespoons fresh lemon juice

2 tablespoons chopped fresh chives

1 tablespoon chopped fresh dill

½ teaspoon garlic salt

½ teaspoon onion powder

¼ teaspoon cracked black pepper

FRIED PICKLES

1 cup all-purpose flour

2 large eggs

½ cup whole milk

1 cup panko bread crumbs

1 teaspoon dried dill

1 teaspoon garlic powder

1 teaspoon kosher salt, plus more for sprinkling

Vegetable oil, for frying

4 **For the dressing:** In a medium bowl, whisk together the buttermilk, mayonnaise, lemon juice, chives, dill, garlic salt, onion powder, and pepper. Adjust the seasoning to taste. The dressing can be stored in the refrigerator in an airtight container for up to 1 week.

5 **For the fried pickles:** Set a wire rack over a baking sheet lined with paper towels.

6 In a large zip-top plastic bag, combine the drained quick pickles and flour and shake until the pickles are well coated. In a bowl, whisk together the eggs and milk. In a shallow dish, combine the panko, dill, garlic powder, and salt. Working in batches, dip the floured pickle chips into the egg mixture, and then toss them in the seasoned panko, fully coating them.

7 In a large heavy skillet or cast-iron pan set over medium-high heat, heat ½ inch of oil until it reaches 350°F.

8 Working in batches, shallow-fry the pickles until they are golden brown, 1 to 2 minutes per side. Transfer the pickles to the rack to drain and immediately sprinkle them with kosher salt.

9 Serve the fried pickles hot, with the dressing on the side.

QUICK VEGETABLE PICKLES This brine is great for pickling a variety of other vegetables, such as sugar snap peas (one of my favorites), carrots, fennel, and onions. Try pickled carrots on a roast pork sandwich, pickled fennel in a salad, and pickled onions on tacos. Also, you can reserve the leftover pickling liquid as a punchy addition to vinaigrettes—I like to replace half of the vinegar called for in a vinaigrette recipe with brine to mix things up.

QUICK-PICKLING

I grew up pickling the traditional way: boiling filled and sealed jars to ensure many months of preservation. But that process requires equipment and time that I no longer have. Then I discovered quick-pickling, which mimics the tangy flavors and textures of put-up pickles in a fraction of the time, especially when you make small batches instead of trying to pickle the whole garden to save for winter. Consider yourself forewarned, however: Once you start quick-pickling, you might not be able to stop. That is why in certain pickle-focused parts of the country there are some unusual pickles—watermelon rind is a favorite—because the simple process makes just about anything taste good.

Here are some pointers to get you going:

MAKE A SIMPLE QUICK-PICKLE BRINE. When it comes to making pickle juice or brine, there's no specific formula. Most often I use almost equal parts vinegar (or citrus juice) and water, slightly favoring the acid. In some cases, I use all vinegar for a stronger flavor and faster results. Make enough of the vinegar-water solution to cover whatever you're pickling, then add sugar to balance the tartness, kosher salt to season, and any other flavoring agents of your choice, like whole spices, the stems of herbs, and chiles. Start with this basic recipe, and adjust to taste: 2 cups vinegar, 1½ cups water, ½ cup sugar, 2 tablespoons kosher salt, and a tablespoon or two of spices like mustard seeds or peppercorns.

BRING THE BRINE TO A BOIL to marry the flavors, remove from the heat, and pour over your vegetables. Try cucumbers, chiles, sugar snap peas, carrots, shallots, onions, peaches, tomatoes, beets, turnips, or okra. Because the brine is hot, it will soften your vegetables slightly.

LET STEEP FOR 15 TO 20 MINUTES. Your pickles are now ready to eat! (If you prefer a super-crunchy pickle, cool the brine after bringing it to a boil, but anticipate waiting a few days before eating, so the brine has a chance to fully infuse the vegetables.)

Quick pickles will keep covered in the refrigerator for up to 1 week.

FENNEL AND SAUSAGE
STUFFED
MUSHROOMS

SERVES **12** • PREP **25 minutes** • COOK **30 minutes**

Stuffed mushrooms are really all about the filling. As far as I'm concerned, the mushroom is just a vehicle for this hearty sausage and rich cream cheese combination, which guarantees that each bite will be packed with a punch. The fennel adds a sweet, mild anise flavor and complexity to the filling, but if you don't have the vegetable on hand, simply omit it. These can be completely assembled in advance and then popped into the oven right before serving, making them perfect for entertaining. Fair warning that these don't last long—they seem to disappear as quickly as you plate them up!

24 large cremini mushrooms

1 pound sweet Italian sausage, casings removed

½ cup chopped fennel (optional)

2 bunches scallions, chopped (white and green parts kept separate)

1 (8-ounce) package cream cheese, at room temperature

½ cup grated Parmesan cheese, plus more for topping

¼ cup seasoned dry bread crumbs

½ teaspoon kosher salt

¼ teaspoon cracked black pepper

1 Preheat the oven to 350°F. Line a baking sheet with parchment paper.

2 Clean the mushrooms caps with a damp paper towel. Carefully break off the stems and, using the tip of a spoon, hollow out the interior of the mushroom cap to create a bigger cavity.

3 Heat a large skillet over medium-high heat. Add the sausage and cook, breaking it up with a wooden spoon, until browned, about 5 minutes. Transfer the sausage to a paper towel–lined plate and let cool.

4 Add the fennel and scallion whites to the skillet and cook until fragrant, about 2 minutes. Transfer to the plate with the sausage and let cool.

5 When the sausage and the fennel mixture are no longer hot, transfer it all to a large bowl. Stir in the cream cheese, Parmesan, bread crumbs, salt, and pepper. The mixture should be very thick. Fill each mushroom cap with a generous amount of the stuffing.

6 Arrange the mushroom caps on the prepared baking sheet. Top with additional Parmesan. (The mushrooms can be made up to this point and refrigerated for up to 24 hours.) Bake until the mushrooms are piping hot and liquid starts to form underneath them, about 20 minutes.

7 To serve, garnish with the scallion greens.

finding inspiration outside of your kitchen

Chances are that if you love cooking, you probably love and appreciate a really good restaurant meal. When you're enjoying a meal out, take the time to observe the details. Take note of what's listed on the menu and observe the way that ingredients are paired together. When I have a great dish at a restaurant, I'll take those details home with me to re-create something that mimics the incredible meal that I've just had. It's a great way to exercise your creative chops in the kitchen. I find that this is particularly relevant when traveling and tasting the local fare; I go as far as keeping a food log on trips, detailing what I had and what was so good about it. Re-creating some fantastic food memories that were made while traveling is a great way to remember good times and reinvent your own cooking repertoire.

GLAZED BUFFALO CHICKEN WINGS

WITH BUTTERMILK– BLUE CHEESE DRESSING

DRESSING

½ cup mayonnaise

2 tablespoons buttermilk

2 tablespoons fresh lemon juice

½ cup crumbled blue cheese

2 tablespoons minced fresh chives

½ teaspoon garlic salt

½ teaspoon onion powder

¼ teaspoon cracked black pepper

Kosher salt

Chicken wings have recently found their way onto my list of favorite foods to cook at home. Call me a late bloomer, but I just never considered making these at home until the last couple of years—and when I did, I really fell for them. Who knew that they were so easy and versatile? Their laid-back nature makes them perfect for watching the big game, having friends over, or throwing together a quick casual meal for my husband and me. This recipe has a great balance of sweet and heat, and the honey adds a nice sticky glaze. This broil-and-toss method is the only way I make wings now—it's quick, and cleanup is a cinch. The buttermilk–blue cheese dressing is a classic, cool accompaniment to the kick of the wings. I often double the dressing when I make it, saving the extra to use as a salad dressing during the week.

SERVES 4 • PREP 20 minutes • COOK 25 minutes

1 **For the dressing:** In a medium bowl, whisk together the mayonnaise, buttermilk, lemon juice, blue cheese, chives, garlic salt, onion powder, and pepper. Season to taste with salt. The dressing can be stored in an airtight container in the refrigerator for up to 1 week.

continued

WINGS

12 whole chicken wings, wing tips removed, split at the joints

¼ cup vegetable oil

1 teaspoon kosher salt

1 teaspoon cracked black pepper

6 tablespoons (¾ stick) unsalted butter

½ cup hot sauce (I use Frank's RedHot)

¼ cup honey

¼ cup white wine vinegar

Celery sticks, for serving

2 **For the wings:** Put the oven rack in the lower third of the oven. Preheat the broiler. Arrange a wire rack over a rimmed baking sheet.

3 In a large bowl, toss the chicken wings with the oil, salt, and pepper. Arrange the wings on the wire rack and broil, turning after 15 minutes, until golden brown, crisp, and cooked through, about 25 minutes total. Let cool slightly.

4 Meanwhile, in a small saucepan set over medium heat, melt the butter. Add the hot sauce, honey, and vinegar and bring to a simmer. Remove the pan from the heat and pour the mixture into an extra-large bowl.

5 Add the wings to the bowl of sauce and toss until well coated. Transfer to a platter and serve with the celery sticks and blue cheese dressing.

GRILLED FLATBREAD

SERVES **4** • PREP **20 minutes plus rising time** • COOK **35 minutes**

1¾ cups warm water
(105° to 110°F)

1 (.25-ounce) envelope
active dry yeast
(2¼ teaspoons)

2 teaspoons sugar

3 tablespoons
extra-virgin olive oil

4 cups bread flour, plus
more for dusting

2 teaspoons kosher salt

Cooking spray

This flatbread dough is meant for grilling, indoors or out. It stands up well to high heat, resulting in a crispy exterior with beautiful grill marks and a chewy interior in no time at all. (See page 41 for more details on working with yeast dough.) Then the fun really starts! Whether you're entertaining or making a week-night meal, you can set out several ready-to-eat options for top-pings and let everyone customize their flatbread. Try an array of cheeses, thinly sliced or precooked seasonal vegetables, salad greens, and meats like salami and spicy ham (see the variations on pages 65 and 66 for some of my favorite combinations). For a party, you can grill and top the flatbreads, then cut them into bite-size pieces.

1 In a liquid measuring cup, combine the warm water, yeast, and sugar. Let sit until the yeast is bubbly and looks creamy, about 5 minutes. Add the oil.

2 In the bowl of a stand mixer fitted with the paddle attachment, mix together the flour and salt. Gradually pour in the yeast mixture. As the dough begins to come together, switch to the dough hook attachment. Mix, adding a bit more flour if needed, until the dough pulls away from the sides of the bowl, 1 to 3 minutes. You should be able to touch the dough and not have it stick to your fingers. Dust a work surface with flour. Turn the dough out onto the surface and, using floured hands, knead it for 1 to 2 minutes. Shape the dough into a ball. Coat a large bowl with cooking spray. Transfer the dough

continued

to the bowl, cover with a clean kitchen towel or plastic wrap, and let rise in a warm place until doubled in size, about 1 hour.

3 Preheat a grill or cast-iron grill pan to medium-high heat.

4 Punch the dough down, turn it out onto a floured work surface, and divide it into 4 equal pieces. Stretch and press each piece with your hands to form a thin rectangle about ¼ inch thick. If you need to, pick up the dough and let the weight of the dough stretch itself out. It doesn't need to be perfect—it's actually better when it's not. Brush one side of the dough with oil and lay that side down on the preheated grill or grill pan. Cook the dough until it is charred and has a crisp texture, about 5 minutes. Brush the second side with oil, flip, and cook for 3 more minutes. Remove the bread from the grill and cook the remaining dough. You're ready to top it as you please.

GRILLED VEGGIE FLATBREAD WITH BALSAMIC GLAZE In a small saucepan set over medium heat, bring ½ cup balsamic vinegar and 1 tablespoon Worcestershire sauce to a simmer. Simmer until thickened to a glaze, 3 to 5 minutes.

Preheat a grill or grill pan to medium-high heat. Thickly slice a medium zucchini, a yellow squash, a red bell pepper, and a red onion and brush the slices with olive oil. Put the vegetables on the grill and cook until they have grill marks and are softened and caramelized, 6 to 8 minutes total. Remove the vegetables from the grill, let cool slightly, season with salt and pepper, and chop. Grill the flatbreads as directed above.

To serve, spread ⅔ cup store-bought pesto onto 4 hot grilled flatbreads and layer with 6 ounces fresh mozzarella slices. Top evenly with the hot grilled veggies. Drizzle the balsamic glaze over the grilled vegetables and serve.

continued

SMOKED BACON AND FIG FLATBREAD Spread 2 cups (16 ounces) herbed goat cheese over 4 grilled flatbreads. Top with 1 cup arugula and ¼ cup fresh lemon juice and season liberally with salt and pepper. Arrange 12 sliced fresh figs over the tops. Sprinkle with ½ pound (12 slices) smoked bacon that has been cooked until crisp and crumbled.

MARGHERITA PIZZA You can also make grilled pizzas with this dough. For each of the 4 dough rectangles, grill the dough as directed on the first side. Flip, then immediately spread each rectangle with ½ cup Essential Tomato Sauce (page 95), ¼ pound sliced fresh mozzarella cheese, and 4 to 6 fresh basil leaves. Cover the pan or grill while the second side cooks to help melt the cheese. Serve the pizzas hot.

japanese mandoline

When it comes to vegetable and fruit prep, having a Japanese mandoline in your kitchen is a serious timesaver. Very quickly, you can have paper-thin slices of any firm veggie or fruit (or even cheese) ready to be tossed into a salad, roasting pan, or stir-fry. For less than $25, it will more than pay for itself; plus it is small, compact, and really easy to clean. (The French varieties are costlier but not better.) Once you get one, you'll see why they are a workhorse in professional kitchens. One word of caution: The super-sharp blade is what achieves those perfectly thin slices, so do take care to handle it properly and carefully. Use the guard that comes with it and work at a comfortable speed.

CARAMELIZED ONION–TOMATO JAM

My homemade tomato jam packs a very flavorful punch. This delicious and unique sweet-savory condiment is made up of ingredients like molasses, allspice, and chipotle powder to invoke deep smoky flavors. A little goes a long way when incorporated into recipes like the Ratatouille Tart on page 68 or simply served with cheese and crackers, eggs, or on top of grilled chicken or fish. At the height of tomato season, I love to make an extra-big batch and use this as a gift from the kitchen for friends and family.

MAKES 2½ cups · PREP 15 minutes · COOK 1 hour 5 minutes

2 tablespoons
extra-virgin olive oil

2 sweet onions, thinly
sliced

2 teaspoons kosher salt

2 garlic cloves, minced

10 plum tomatoes (about
2½ pounds), seeded and
roughly chopped

½ cup molasses

½ cup apple cider
vinegar

½ cup packed light
brown sugar

½ teaspoon ground
allspice

½ teaspoon ground
cinnamon

½ teaspoon chipotle
powder

1 In a large deep skillet set over medium heat, heat the oil. Add the onions and salt. Cover and cook until the onions are wilted and soft, about 10 minutes. Uncover, reduce the heat to medium-low, and cook, stirring often, until the onions are golden and caramelized, about 20 minutes more.

2 Stir in the garlic and cook for 1 to 2 minutes. Add the tomatoes and cook for 10 minutes.

3 Add the molasses, vinegar, brown sugar, allspice, cinnamon, and chipotle powder. Bring the mixture to a boil, then reduce the heat to medium-low. Cook, stirring frequently, until the tomatoes break down and the jam becomes thick, about 20 minutes. (The jam will keep in an airtight container in the refrigerator for up to 1 week.)

RATATOUILLE
TART

1 sheet frozen puff
pastry, thawed

All-purpose flour, for
dusting

¾ cup Caramelized
Onion–Tomato Jam
(page 67)

3 plum tomatoes, cut into
¼-inch-thick slices

1 Japanese eggplant, cut
into ¼-inch-thick slices

1 yellow squash, cut into
¼-inch-thick slices

1 zucchini, cut into
¼-inch-thick slices

2 roasted red peppers,
thinly sliced

2 to 3 tablespoons extra-
virgin olive oil

Kosher salt and cracked
black pepper

1 tablespoon chopped
fresh oregano

½ cup (2 ounces)
crumbled goat cheese

My freezer is never without a box of frozen puff pastry. With it, I can pull together a sweet or savory tart in no time. The combination of beautifully arranged, delicate layers of vegetables and homemade Caramelized Onion–Tomato Jam makes this recipe something special. I love to serve this as an appetizer for a small party or as part of an afternoon lunch.

1 Preheat the oven to 400°F. Line a baking sheet with parchment paper.

2 On a lightly floured surface, using a rolling pin, roll the sheet of puff pastry into a rectangle that's about 12 × 10½ inches. Transfer the pastry to the prepared baking sheet. Using the tines of a fork, press around the edges of the pastry to form a ½-inch border and then poke a few holes in the center as well. This will prevent the dough from rising too much in the center as it cooks.

3 Spread the jam evenly over the pastry, excluding the border. Layer the tomatoes, eggplant, yellow squash, and zucchini on top in overlapping rows. Sprinkle the roasted red peppers on top of the tart. Drizzle with a little of the oil and brush oil on the tart's edges. Season with salt and pepper, and sprinkle with half of the oregano.

4 Bake until the pastry is golden brown and puffed, 20 to 25 minutes. Remove the pan from the oven and immediately sprinkle the tart with the goat cheese and the remaining oregano. Serve hot.

QUICK RATATOUILLE TART If you are crunched for time, consider swapping the Caramelized Onion–Tomato Jam for an additional 8 ounces herbed goat cheese that can be spread over the puff pastry before topping with the vegetables and baking. It's a quicker way to pull this recipe together that still lets the veggies shine.

SALADS

SUMMER POTATO SALAD 72

PICKLED CUCUMBER SALAD 73

CHARRED CORN SALAD WITH BASIL VINAIGRETTE 74

ESSENTIAL EVERYDAY TOSSED GREEN SALAD, WITH VARIATIONS 76

GRILLED VEGGIE PANZANELLA WITH MOZZARELLA AND BASIL 79

STONE FRUIT SALAD WITH SHERRY VINAIGRETTE AND ROASTED ALMONDS 80

CILANTRO LIME SLAW 81

SUMMER BEAN, PEA, AND RADISH SALAD 82

FUSILLI CAESAR SALAD 85

GRILLED FRUIT SKEWERS WITH CHILI AND LIME 87

TARRAGON CHICKEN SALAD WITH GRAPES 88

GREEK SHRIMP AND ORZO SALAD 89

CHOPPED COBB SALAD 90

CHARRED CORN SALAD

WITH BASIL VINAIGRETTE

CORN

6 ears corn, shucked

Canola oil

Kosher salt and cracked black pepper

BASIL VINAIGRETTE

1½ cups packed fresh basil leaves

1 garlic clove, grated

¼ cup apple cider vinegar

¼ cup extra-virgin olive oil

Kosher salt and cracked black pepper

1 (10-ounce) container small heirloom cherry tomatoes, halved (about 2 cups)

½ small red onion, finely chopped

My mom makes a version of this salad every summer. I'll never forget just how sweet the locally grown corn on the cob is. She often tosses in whole fresh basil, but I like to put the herb into a vibrant green vinaigrette that gets even better as it sits. The salad really does become more flavorful over time, so I like to make it a few hours in advance before serving—this makes it perfect for a summer picnic or barbecue. For an even easier version of this summer salad, you can use leftover ears of cooked corn. Simply skip the step where you char the corn on the grill and instead cut the kernels off the precooked cobs.

SERVES **6 to 8** • PREP **20 minutes** • COOK **15 minutes**

1 **For the corn:** Preheat a grill pan or outdoor grill to high heat.

2 Brush or rub each corn cob with the canola oil and sprinkle with salt and pepper. Put the corn on the grill and char each side, 2 to 3 minutes per side. Set aside until cool enough to handle, about 5 minutes. Stand each ear up, stalk end down, in a wide, shallow bowl and, using a knife, slice the corn kernels off the cob. Set aside.

3 **For the vinaigrette:** In a food processor or blender, pulse the basil and garlic until the basil starts to break down. Add the vinegar. Continue pulsing while adding the oil in a steady stream, then process until smooth. Season with salt and pepper.

4 In a large bowl, combine the corn, tomatoes, and red onion. Drizzle the basil vinaigrette over the vegetables and toss well to coat. Season to taste with salt and pepper. Serve at room temperature or chilled.

ESSENTIAL EVERYDAY
TOSSED GREEN SALAD

WITH VARIATIONS

SERVES **4** • PREP **15 minutes**

I'm crazy about a fresh, crisp green salad alongside a weeknight dinner. When executed right, a simple salad—just greens and a flavorful vinaigrette or dressing—can be perfection and says a lot about the cook who is preparing it. From there, it's easy to build a heartier salad, if you like, by adding vegetables, fruits, cheeses, and nuts. Use this basic formula as a guide for customizing your own tossed salads. I like letting the seasons dictate what ends up in the bowl. Adding whatever fruits and vegetables are ripe will result in vibrant flavor, texture, and color that can't be matched by any salad that comes from a bag.

8 cups salad greens (mesclun mix, butter lettuce, romaine, etc.), chopped or torn if necessary

1½ to 2 cups fresh fruits and/or veggies (radishes, fennel, pears, figs, orange or grapefruit segments, etc.) or ⅓ cup dried fruit (cranberries, cherries, etc.)

½ cup crumbled or cubed cheese (Parmesan, fresh mozzarella, blue cheese, etc.)

⅓ cup nuts or seeds (almonds, pecans, walnuts, pepitas, sunflower seeds), toasted (see page 203)

½ cup dressing of choice (see pages 49, 56, 60, 74, 80, 82, and 85)

1 Put the salad greens in a large serving bowl twice the size of your salad to make tossing easier.

2 Choose and prepare your other salad ingredients from the list, aiming for a pleasing mix of tastes, colors, and textures. You can grill or roast the ingredients as well as using them raw. Chop, slice, or shred your ingredients so that they are bite-size. Add these to the greens in the bowl.

3 If the salad will be eaten right away, toss the salad with the dressing and serve. If you will be serving it later, assemble the salad but reserve the dressing, adding it and tossing just before the meal.

GARDEN SALAD WITH BLUE CHEESE Butter lettuce, blanched haricots verts, heirloom tomatoes, Maytag blue cheese, toasted walnuts, and Sherry Vinaigrette (page 80).

BEET, APPLE, AND GOAT CHEESE SALAD Mesclun greens, sliced roasted red and yellow beets, chopped Granny Smith apple, crumbled goat cheese, sliced pecans, and Basil Vinaigrette (page 74).

MEDITERRANEAN SALAD Chopped romaine, quartered marinated artichoke hearts, diced roasted red bell peppers, chopped pepperoncini peppers, sliced red onion, crumbled feta cheese, and Mustard Vinaigrette (page 82)

knives

Good sharp knives may be the most important tools with which to arm yourself as a home cook. They're definitely one of the best investments you'll make for your kitchen. Purchasing knives in a set can get very expensive and the majority of those knives may never make it out of the knife block; I tend to use just a few knives over and over, for example. One of the most important things to do before purchasing good-quality knives is to actually hold them in your hand. A knife should feel comfortable—not too heavy or too light. It's even better if the store will let you try out the knife there before purchasing. A knife skills class could be another opportunity to work with several different brands and styles to determine which is the best fit for you. Once you've made the investment, take good care of them and have them sharpened every six months or so at a kitchen supply store or by your local butcher.

My advice would be to invest in the following, at the best quality you can afford:

PARING KNIFE: Perfect for smaller, more precise tasks like trimming and peeling vegetables and fruit.

CHEF'S KNIFE: My go-to knife for most things, including chopping vegetables and herbs and cutting meat. I use a 10-inch knife because I've got small hands, but anything from an 8-inch to 14-inch chef's knife will work—choose whatever size is most comfortable for you.

SERRATED KNIFE: Great for slicing bread and sturdy ingredients like winter squash, as well as delicate ones like tomatoes.

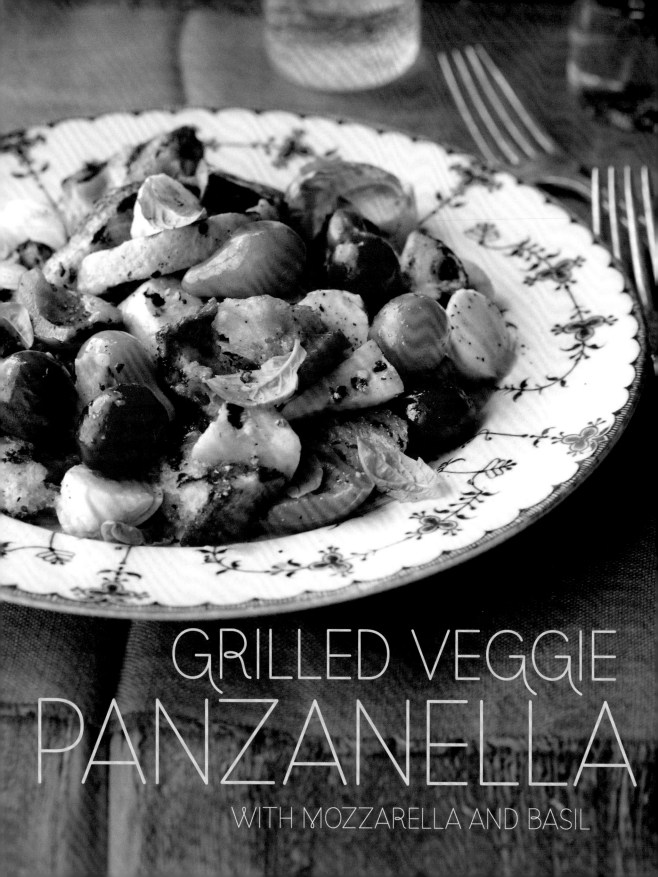

GRILLED VEGGIE
PANZANELLA
WITH MOZZARELLA AND BASIL

Cooking spray (optional)

1 loaf French bread, cut on an angle into 1-inch-thick slices

½ cup extra-virgin olive oil, plus more for brushing and drizzling

Kosher salt and cracked black pepper

1 yellow squash, cut on an angle into ¾-inch-thick slices

1 small zucchini, cut on an angle into ¾-inch-thick slices

1 orange bell pepper, cut into quarters

8 ounces heirloom cherry tomatoes

½ cup red wine vinegar

½ teaspoon Dijon mustard

1 garlic clove, grated

8 ounces fresh mozzarella cheese, cut into ½-inch dice

1 cup fresh basil leaves, torn

After you make your first bread salad, you will never look back. The simple method of toasting the bread to get it crispy enough to then soak up a vibrant vinaigrette results in so much flavor. As the seasons change throughout the year, I like customizing the panzanella to highlight what is freshest at the market. Consider roasting the vegetables or serving them raw in this salad, too. The end result is always colorful and so easy to put together.

1 Preheat a grill or grill pan to medium-high heat. If using an outdoor grill, coat a grill basket with cooking spray and put it on the grill.

2 Brush both sides of the bread with oil and season with salt and pepper. Grill until grill marks appear, about 2 minutes per side. When cool enough to handle, cut or tear into 1-inch cubes.

3 In a large bowl, combine the squash, zucchini, and bell pepper. Drizzle with oil, season with salt and black pepper, and toss to coat. Grill, flipping once, until the vegetables have grill marks and are softened and caramelized, 6 to 8 minutes. When cool enough to handle, cut the squash, zucchini, and pepper into 1-inch pieces and transfer to another large bowl. Add the tomatoes to the first bowl, drizzle with a little more oil, and season with salt and pepper. Grill (if outdoors, use the grill basket) and cook until charred and caramelized, 4 to 5 minutes. Add the tomatoes to the grilled vegetables.

4 In a small bowl, combine the vinegar, mustard, and garlic. While whisking, slowly drizzle in the ½ cup oil and whisk until emulsified. Season with salt and pepper.

5 Add the toasted bread and mozzarella to the bowl of vegetables. Drizzle in the vinaigrette, add the torn basil leaves, and toss well. Let stand for 10 minutes before serving to allow the flavors to develop.

SUMMER
BEAN, PEA, AND RADISH
SALAD

This unique salad has a bright fresh flavor thanks to the combination of greens, herbs, and cooked and raw vegetables. Blanching the beans and peas in boiling salted water and then quickly cooling them in ice water is crucial as it gives them a great crisp-tender bite, a vibrant color, and just the right seasoning. The sweet flavor of fresh peas is so important in this salad, though you can substitute frozen petite peas that have been thawed, if you must. The peppery radishes and arugula provide a great punch. Finally, the colors of this beautiful salad are sure to steal the show at the dinner table.

SERVES **4 to 6** • PREP **20 minutes** • COOK **15 minutes**

MUSTARD VINAIGRETTE

1 medium to large shallot, minced

1 garlic clove, grated

2 teaspoons finely chopped fresh tarragon

1 tablespoon whole-grain mustard

¼ cup sherry vinegar

¼ cup extra-virgin olive oil

Kosher salt and cracked black pepper

SALAD

¾ pound green beans, stem ends trimmed

¾ pound yellow wax beans, stem ends trimmed

½ cup shelled fresh peas

4 cups loosely packed arugula

6 large radishes, cut into ⅛-inch-thick slices

1 **For the vinaigrette:** In a small bowl, combine the shallot, garlic, tarragon, mustard, and vinegar. Whisking constantly, slowly drizzle in the oil and whisk until the dressing is emulsified. Season with salt and pepper.

2 **For the salad:** Bring a large pot of salted water to a boil. Prepare an ice bath (a large bowl of cold water and ice).

3 Add the green and yellow wax beans to the boiling salted water and cook until blanched (tender but still crisp), about 3 minutes. Remove the beans with a spider or slotted spoon and plunge them into the ice bath to cold-shock them (stop the cooking). Drain and dry them completely. In the same pot of boiling water, blanch the peas for 1 minute and then shock them in the ice bath. Drain and dry them completely.

4 Arrange the arugula on a serving platter. Scatter the blanched beans and peas and the radishes on top, and drizzle with the vinaigrette. Toss and serve.

BLANCHING

I'm a firm believer that we eat with our eyes first, and no other technique will make your food look better and brighter than blanching. Primarily used with vegetables, blanching sets the vegetables' color, and at the same time quickly tenderizes them. This precooking makes the vegetables ready to go into a gratin, for example, where harder vegetables need a little head start from blanching so they will cook faster and more evenly. Blanching is a great help when hosting a party, too; blanching quick-cooking vegetables ahead of time means you can sauté them just long enough to heat them up and add flavor. This quick dip in rolling boiling water will also loosen the skins of foods like tomatoes or peaches, making it easy to slip them right off, saving time when you're making big-batch recipes like homemade jam or tomato sauce. Use this technique, too, before you freeze fresh vegetables, as they will retain all of their nutrients in addition to their beautiful color.

- Bring a pot of salted water to a rolling boil.

- Meanwhile, create an ice bath by filling a large bowl with ice and water.

- Trim, clean, and cut, if needed, the food that will be blanched.

- Add the food to the boiling water for as short as 30 seconds but no longer than a few minutes—just until brightly colored and crisp-tender.

- Remove the food from the boiling water with a slotted spoon or drain in a colander, then transfer to the ice bath. The ice-cold water will shock the food and stop the cooking process. (Alternatively, if you don't have enough ice to make an ice bath, rinse the food immediately in the coldest water possible.) When the vegetables are cool, drain them and proceed with your recipe or dry them completely and freeze.

FUSILLI
CAESAR SALAD

CAESAR DRESSING

⅓ cup mayonnaise

¼ cup fresh lemon juice

2 tablespoons extra-virgin olive oil

2 teaspoons Dijon mustard

1 teaspoon Worcestershire sauce

½ cup grated Parmesan cheese

2 garlic cloves, minced or grated

1 anchovy fillet, rinsed, dried, and roughly chopped

Kosher salt and cracked black pepper

SALAD

1 pound fusilli pasta, cooked al dente, rinsed, drained, and chilled

2 romaine hearts, cut crosswise into ½-inch pieces

1 cup grated Parmesan cheese, plus a small chunk for shaving (optional)

Kosher salt and cracked black pepper

This salad is a go-to option for me for picnics, potlucks, and even a quick weeknight dinner. Adding the fusilli is an excellent way to make a traditional Caesar salad a bit more filling and interesting; the pasta adds a substance and body to the dish that a crouton just can't muster. When I serve this for dinner, I like to pick up a rotisserie chicken from the grocery store, shred it, and toss it in. The homemade dressing is the star of the dish—and without the traditional raw egg yolks, it's perfect for everyone to eat. Recently I made a huge bowl of this for a rooftop party and served it alongside pizza that we had picked up from the local pizzeria—it was a great pairing and incredibly easy to pull off for a big group.

SERVES **4 to 6** • PREP **15 minutes** • COOK **15 minutes**

1 **For the dressing:** In a blender or food processor, combine the mayonnaise, lemon juice, oil, mustard, Worcestershire sauce, Parmesan, garlic, anchovy, and salt and pepper to taste. Process until emulsified and smooth. Refrigerate until ready to use. Any extra dressing should be refrigerated and used within 3 days.

2 **For the salad:** In a large bowl, toss the pasta, romaine, and Parmesan with the dressing. Season to taste with salt and pepper. Shave Parmesan over the salad, if desired, and serve.

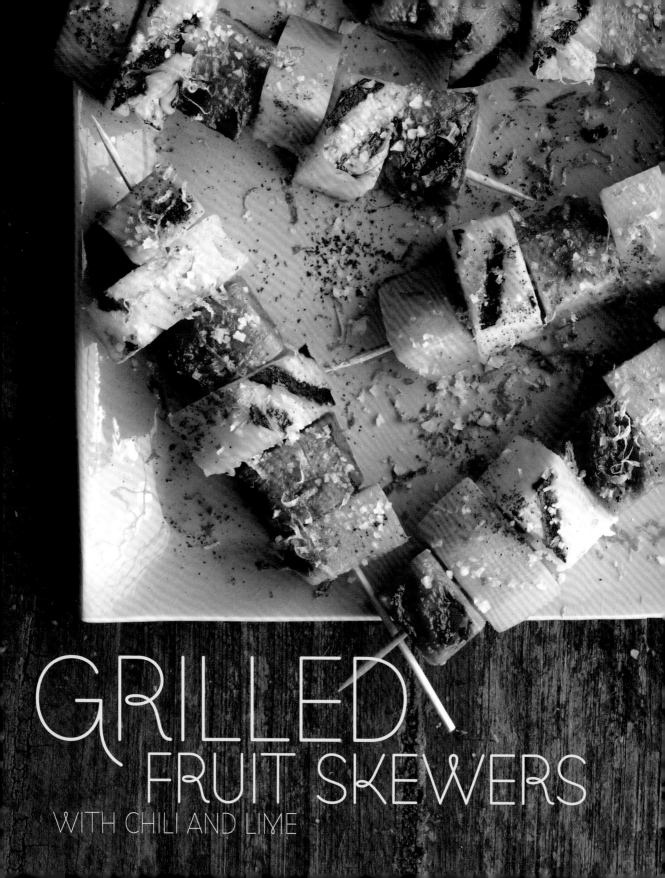

GRILLED
FRUIT SKEWERS
WITH CHILI AND LIME

½ (5- to 6-pound)
seedless watermelon

1 pineapple

2 mangoes

Grated zest and juice of
1 lime

Vegetable oil, for
brushing

2 teaspoons chili powder

1 teaspoon coarse sea
salt, plus more for
serving (optional)

Lime wedges, for serving
(optional)

18 skewers (if wooden,
soak in water for
20 minutes prior to use)

It wasn't until I moved to NYC that I discovered the ideal pick-me-up for a hot day: fruit wedges sprinkled with lime and chili powder. From June through August you can find vendors on street corners dedicated to this unexpected Mexican treat. To take the flavor one note further, I skewer the fruit and toss it onto the grill to develop smoky grill marks that play well with the sweetness of the watermelon, pineapple, and mangoes.

1 Remove the rind of the watermelon, the skin and eyes of the pineapple, and the peels and pits of the mangoes and discard. Split the pineapple in quarters lengthwise and cut out and discard the hard core. Cut all the fruit into 1-inch cubes and thread them onto the skewers. Put the skewers in a large zip-top plastic bag, being careful not to puncture the bag. Add the lime juice, toss gently to incorporate, and seal. Refrigerate for at least 30 minutes, or until ready to use.

2 Preheat a grill or grill pan to medium-high heat.

3 Remove the skewers from the plastic bag and place them on a baking sheet. Brush the fruit with oil and put the skewers on the grill. Grill the fruit on both sides until grill marks appear and the fruit begins to caramelize, 6 to 8 minutes total. Transfer to a serving platter.

4 In a small bowl, combine the lime zest, chili powder, and sea salt. Sprinkle the seasoning over the grilled fruit. Serve with lime wedges and additional sea salt, if desired.

GRILLED FRUIT WITH ICE CREAM If grilling fruit piques your interest, consider grilling stone fruits like peaches or plums. Skip the marinating step, but do brush the pitted halves with a little vegetable oil. When not too ripe, stone fruits hold up really well on the grill and the process caramelizes the natural sugars in them. Pair them with ice cream instead of chili, salt, and lime for a divine dessert.

CHOPPED
COBB SALAD

½ head romaine lettuce, cut crosswise into ½-inch pieces

½ head Boston lettuce, cut into ½-inch pieces

½ pound roast turkey breast, cut into ½-inch cubes (about 2 cups)

6 slices bacon, cooked and crumbled

2 avocados, cut into ½-inch cubes

4 vine-ripened tomatoes, seeded and cut into ½-inch cubes

¾ cup (3 ounces) crumbled blue cheese

2 hard-boiled large eggs, cut into ½-inch cubes

Buttermilk–Blue Cheese Dressing (page 60)

¼ cup finely chopped fresh chives

When I was going to culinary school in Los Angeles, I fell in love with a place called Toast that served the most delicious salads I'd ever had. They had a variety to choose from, and many of them were served chopped. Being in cooking school, I was in a frame of mind to really appreciate knife work, and I swear that having everything in those big salad bowls be uniform in size made the end result taste even better. Cobb salad is a classic, and serving it chopped and tossed in homemade Buttermilk–Blue Cheese Dressing ensures that every bite is balanced taste-wise, while still retaining its beautiful texture and crunch. And with the added protein from the roast turkey, crispy bacon, and hard-boiled eggs, it's also hearty enough to make a meal.

In a large bowl, combine the lettuces and toss with the turkey, bacon, avocados, tomatoes, blue cheese, and eggs. Just before serving, pour the dressing over the salad and toss. Garnish with fresh chives.

SANDWICHES & SOUPS

SHRIMP ROLLS

3 pounds medium shrimp, peeled and deveined

¾ cup mayonnaise

1 small bunch scallions, finely chopped

Grated zest and juice of 2 lemons

¼ teaspoon celery salt

¼ teaspoon garlic salt

2 ribs celery, finely chopped, celery leaves reserved

8 split-top hot dog buns

¼ cup (½ stick) unsalted butter, melted

This recipe captures everything I love about lobster rolls, yet is easier to prepare and easier on your wallet. Sweet shrimp are the star, enhanced by lemon zest, lemon juice, celery salt, and scallions and topped with crisp, bright-tasting celery leaves. If you are pressed for time, the shrimp can be cooked in advance and then mixed with the dressing just before serving to make this recipe come together quickly. But no matter what you do, do not skip the buttery, toasted buns—they are a crucial finishing touch.

1 Bring a large pot of salted water to a boil. Add the shrimp and cook just until they are cooked through and pink, and float to the top, 2 to 3 minutes. Remove the shrimp, rinse with cold water, and drain. Transfer the shrimp to a plate or baking sheet and refrigerate until ready to use.

2 In a medium bowl, combine the mayonnaise, scallions, lemon zest and juice, celery salt, and garlic salt. Stir in the shrimp and chopped celery. Refrigerate for at least 30 minutes or up to 2 hours.

3 Preheat a grill, grill pan, or skillet to medium-high heat.

4 Brush the insides of each bun with melted butter. Put the buns buttered side down on the grill and toast until golden brown or lightly charred, 1 to 2 minutes.

5 Divide the shrimp mixture evenly among the buns. Garnish with the reserved celery leaves and serve.

LOBSTER ROLLS Lobster rolls are an easy variation—just substitute 1½ pounds cooked and roughly chopped lobster meat for the shrimp. Also, swap out the celery salt for 2 teaspoons fresh tarragon, chopped, and ¼ teaspoon kosher salt.

GRILLED
APPLE, BACON, AND CHEDDAR
SANDWICHES

SERVES **4** • PREP **10 minutes** • COOK **20 minutes**

¼ cup (½ stick)
unsalted butter, at room
temperature

8 (½-inch-thick) slices
white bread

4 teaspoons whole-grain
mustard

½ pound cheddar cheese,
shredded (2 cups)

12 slices applewood-
smoked bacon, cooked
until crisp

1 Granny Smith apple,
thinly sliced

I love this sandwich. I make it for lunch when I'm working from home; I make it for dinner for Robby and me; and I even make it when we have guests. A good grilled cheese sandwich is comfort food at its finest: easy to throw together and so tasty. This particular combination of tart green apple slices, smoky bacon, and tangy whole-grain mustard served between crispy bread with melted cheddar cheese is perfectly balanced in flavor and texture. Try it and see for yourself—soon you'll be eating it for breakfast, too.

1 Preheat a grill pan or large skillet over medium-low heat.

2 Butter one side of each slice of bread. Put 4 of the slices on a cutting board, buttered side down, and spread 1 teaspoon of the mustard over the unbuttered side of each. Top the mustard with the cheddar, bacon, and apple, dividing them evenly among the bread slices. Top the sandwiches with the remaining slices of bread, buttered side up.

3 Put the assembled sandwiches on the grill pan. Cook until the cheese begins to melt and the bottom is golden brown, 3 to 5 minutes. Flip and cook the other side until golden brown, about 2 minutes.

4 Remove the sandwiches from the skillet, slice them in half, and serve hot.

PRESSED PICNIC SANDWICH

WITH ROASTED RED PEPPER– PEPPERONCINI SPREAD

SERVES 8 to 10 • **PREP 25 minutes plus chilling time**

SPREAD

½ cup mayonnaise

1 tablespoon fresh lemon juice

3 roasted red peppers, finely chopped

2 to 3 pepperoncini, finely chopped

1 garlic clove, grated

Kosher salt and cracked black pepper

SANDWICH

1 (12- to 14-inch) loaf ciabatta bread, halved horizontally

5 ounces herbed goat cheese

¼ pound prosciutto, thinly sliced

¼ pound salami, thinly sliced

1 cup marinated artichoke hearts, drained and sliced

2 cups arugula

Balsamic vinegar, for drizzling

Kosher salt and cracked black pepper

Our first apartment in New York City was conveniently located just a short walk from Central Park, and knowing that we wouldn't live there forever, we did our best to take advantage of the proximity. This recipe quickly emerged as the ideal picnic sandwich because it can feed a crowd and be made in advance so the flavors have time to come together.

1 **For the spread:** In a small bowl, whisk together the mayonnaise, lemon juice, roasted red peppers, pepperoncini, and garlic. Season to taste with salt and pepper.

2 **For the sandwich:** Scoop out the center of each bread half, creating a hollow space for all the ingredients. Spread the herbed goat cheese on both sides of the bread, and then spread the roasted red pepper and pepperoncini spread on top. On the bottom half of the bread, layer the prosciutto, salami, and artichokes. Top with the arugula, drizzle with balsamic vinegar, and season with salt and pepper. Put the top half of the bread on the sandwich and wrap tightly in plastic wrap. Put the sandwich on a baking sheet and top with another baking sheet. Put a heavy pan (like cast iron) on the top baking sheet and refrigerate for at least 4 hours and up to overnight to allow the flavors to marry. (If you can't fit a baking sheet in your refrigerator, put the sandwich on a large plate or platter and top with the heaviest pan you have.)

3 To serve, unwrap the sandwich and cut it crosswise into 8 to 10 pieces.

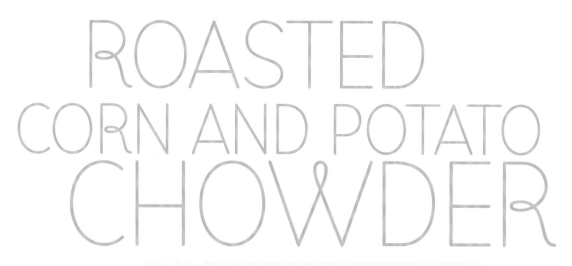

ROASTED CORN AND POTATO CHOWDER

SERVES 6 to 8 • PREP 20 minutes • COOK 1 hour 15 minutes

5 ears corn, shucked

1 pound red potatoes, cut into ½-inch cubes

1 tablespoon extra-virgin olive oil, plus more for drizzling

Kosher salt and cracked black pepper

2 leeks, white and light green parts, chopped

1 poblano pepper, chopped

1 teaspoon fresh thyme leaves

4 cups low-sodium chicken broth

3 cups heavy cream

3 scallions, finely chopped

⅛ teaspoon cayenne pepper

¼ cup chopped red onion

½ avocado, chopped

The secret to this recipe is roasting the corn, which accentuates its sweetness and buttery flavor. The roasted potatoes help to thicken this hearty chowder and round out its flavor. The slight heat from the poblano peppers is a great contrast to the creamy base. I think this chowder is best made in late summer when fresh corn is at its finest, but as the soup freezes beautifully, it's also a great option for a cold day in the fall when chowder is sure to hit the spot.

1 Preheat the oven to 400°F. Put the oven rack in the upper third of the oven.

2 Arrange the corn and potatoes on a large baking sheet. Drizzle liberally with oil and season with salt and pepper. Roast, turning the corn as needed and flipping the potatoes once, until the corn's kernels are plump, about 30 minutes. Turn the oven to broil and broil until the corn and potatoes start to color and turn light brown, 3 to 5 minutes. Let the corn and potatoes cool.

3 Meanwhile, in a large heavy soup pot set over medium heat, heat 1 tablespoon of oil. Add the leeks, poblano, and thyme. Season lightly with salt and pepper and cook, stirring occasionally, until the vegetables are softened and fragrant, about 10 minutes.

4 Cut the kernels off of the cobs and reserve the cobs. Reserving ½ cup corn for garnish, transfer the remainder

to the pot of vegetables. Stir in the roasted potatoes. Add the chicken broth, cream, and reserved cobs and bring to a simmer. Cook until the chowder starts to thicken, about 30 minutes. Remove the cobs and stir in the scallions and cayenne; season to taste with salt and pepper. (The soup will keep in an airtight container in the refrigerator for up to 2 days.)

5 To serve, ladle the chowder into soup bowls and garnish with the reserved roasted corn and the red onion and avocado.

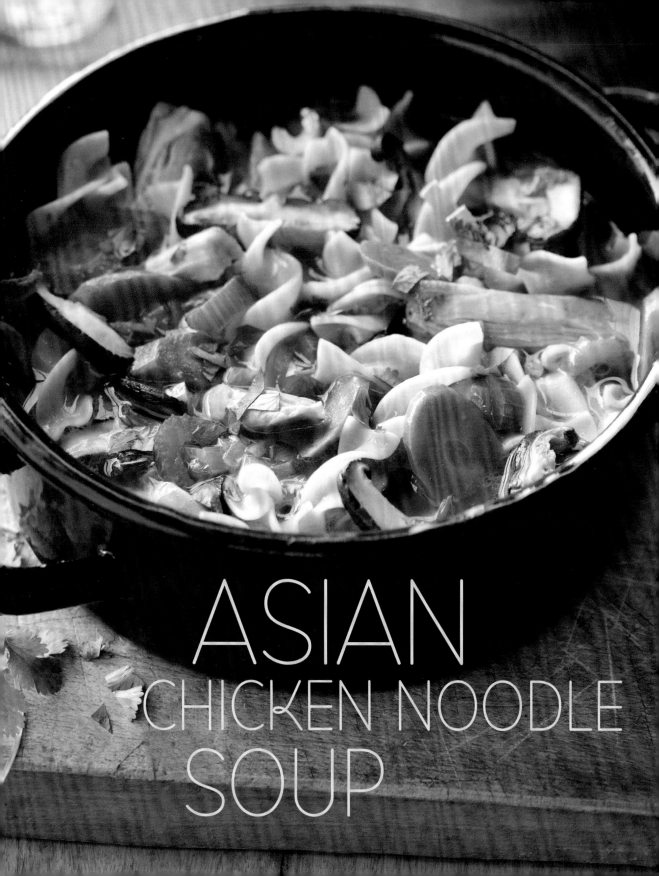

ASIAN
CHICKEN NOODLE
SOUP

2 pounds bone-in, skin-on chicken thighs (about 5 large)

2 tablespoons extra-virgin olive oil

Kosher salt and cracked black pepper

1 tablespoon unsalted butter

1 medium yellow onion, chopped

2 carrots, chopped

2 ribs celery, chopped

1 garlic clove, minced

4 ounces shiitake mushrooms, stemmed and sliced

8 cups low-sodium chicken broth

2 tablespoons white miso

1 (1-inch) piece ginger, peeled and sliced into ¼-inch-thick coins

1¼ cups (4 ounces) wide egg noodles

¼ cup cilantro leaves, roughly chopped

There are few things in life that are more comforting than a big bowl of homemade chicken noodle soup, and every good home cook should have a trusted recipe for this classic dish in her repertoire. Using chicken thighs is key, as the meat is more tender and flavorful than chicken breasts. While the chicken roasts, take the time to prepare the rest of your ingredients so that when it's done, you can put the soup together in no time. Asian-influenced ingredients—miso, ginger, and cilantro—give this soup a flavorful spin, but I stay true to my first love when it comes to the noodles: Old-fashioned, chewy egg noodles are a must.

1 Preheat the oven to 425°F.

2 Arrange the chicken on a rimmed baking sheet and drizzle with the oil. Season liberally with salt and pepper. Roast until the chicken is cooked through and reaches 160°F on a thermometer inserted into the thickest part of the thigh, 30 to 35 minutes. Let the chicken cool slightly, then remove and discard the skin and bones; shred the meat.

3 In a large soup pot set over medium-high heat, melt the butter. Add the onion, carrots, and celery and cook just until the vegetables begin to soften, about 3 minutes. Season with salt and pepper. Add the garlic and cook for 1 minute. Add the mushrooms and cook until softened, about 4 minutes. Add the chicken broth, miso, and ginger, and bring to a simmer. Add the egg noodles and, adjusting the heat as necessary to keep the soup at a simmer, continue cooking until the noodles are cooked through, about 10 minutes. Add the chicken to the soup and cook to heat through. (The soup will keep in an airtight container in the refrigerator for up to 1 day.)

4 To serve, discard the ginger and season the soup to taste with salt and pepper. Ladle into soup bowls and garnish with the cilantro before serving.

SWEET PEA SOUP

If there is one ingredient that you will always find in my freezer, it's frozen petite peas. Delicious as they are, fresh peas are available for only a short season and are really delicate—when bought out of season, many times they are tough and starchy. In general, and for this soup in particular, I recommend buying frozen baby or petite peas, not regular peas, as they are more tender and flavorful. This easy-to-assemble, bright green soup is vibrant, flavorful, and sophisticated, making it perfect for entertaining. You'll have everyone fooled into thinking you've been shelling peas all afternoon to make it—though I've found the fun reaction from my guests after I've disclosed my frozen secret ingredient makes a great dinner conversation and usually prompts a recipe exchange.

SERVES 6 • PREP **20 minutes** • COOK **15 minutes**

¼ cup (½ stick) unsalted butter

1 bunch scallions, finely chopped (white and green parts kept separate)

½ teaspoon sugar

1 teaspoon kosher salt

1½ teaspoons cracked black pepper

1 garlic clove, minced

4 cups low-sodium chicken broth

1 (16-ounce) package frozen petite peas

1 cup heavy cream

Crème fraîche, for garnish (optional)

Pea shoots, for garnish (optional)

1 In a large soup pot set over medium-high heat, melt 3 tablespoons of the butter. Add the scallion whites, sugar, salt, and pepper. Cook, stirring, until just fragrant, about 2 minutes. Add the garlic and cook, stirring, for 1 minute. Add the chicken broth and bring to a simmer, scraping up any bits from the bottom of the pot. Add the peas and half of the scallion greens (reserving the rest for garnish). Simmer until the peas are thawed and tender, about 3 minutes. Remove the pan from the heat and let cool slightly.

2 Using an immersion blender, blend the soup until it's semi-smooth but still has some texture. (Alternatively, puree the soup in batches in a standard blender.)

3 Return the soup pot to medium-high heat. Add the heavy cream and stir well. Cook until the soup is warmed through, 5 to 7 minutes. Remove from the heat and stir in the remaining 1 tablespoon butter until melted. Season to taste with salt and pepper.

4 To serve, ladle the soup into serving bowls and garnish with crème fraîche and pea shoots, if desired.

a serious blender

There are blenders and then there are *blenders*. You know what I'm talking about. I want a blender that will turn golf balls into fairy dust. A serious blender can make ice cream, breads, cakes, salad dressings, sauces, sublimely smooth soups, and fresh fruit and vegetable juices. It's a blast to work with in the kitchen. Admittedly I most often do use mine for making smoothies (now blended together in only 5 seconds flat), but I've also started using my blender for most tasks that I used to use my food processor for. I've rarely met anyone who regrets making the investment in a Vitamix or similar brand. For quick and easy clean up, try this trick: Fill the dirty blender with a couple of cups of hot water and a squirt of dish soap and whiz for a minute or two.

ROASTED TOMATO SOUP
WITH PESTO AND CHEESY CROUTONS

SOUP

3 tablespoons extra-virgin olive oil

1 medium yellow onion, chopped

4 garlic cloves, minced

1 (28-ounce) can San Marzano whole plum tomatoes

2½ cups low-sodium chicken broth

2 tablespoons pesto

2 tablespoons sugar

½ cup heavy cream

Kosher salt and cracked black pepper

CROUTONS

1 (15-inch) loaf day-old French bread, cut into 1-inch cubes

4 tablespoons unsalted butter, melted

Kosher salt and cracked black pepper

¼ pound cheddar cheese, shredded (1 cup)

Tomato soup and grilled cheese go together like bees and honey, and this soup mimics that delicious combination. This simple soup recipe is full of flavor and a great staple, improved only by stirring in a bit of prepared pesto, an easy addition that makes a big difference in taste. The cheesy croutons are made just like any homemade crouton, but are topped with melty cheddar. Each tiny package of toasty bread and sharp cheese scooped up with soup makes the perfect bite in every spoonful.

1 **For the soup:** In a large saucepan or Dutch oven set over medium-high heat, heat 2 tablespoons of the oil. Add the onion and garlic. Cook, stirring frequently, until translucent and fragrant, about 3 minutes. Add the tomatoes and their juices, chicken broth, pesto, and sugar. Use a potato masher to crush the tomatoes. Bring the soup to a simmer and cook for 5 minutes.

2 Using an immersion blender, blend the soup until smooth. (Alternatively, puree the soup in batches in a standard blender.) Stir in the cream, bring the soup just to a simmer, and cook for 10 minutes. Season to taste with salt and pepper. (The soup will keep in an airtight container in the refrigerator for up to 3 days.)

3 **For the croutons:** Preheat the oven to 325°F. Line a baking sheet with foil or parchment paper.

4 In a medium bowl, toss the bread cubes with the melted butter. Season liberally with salt and pepper. Spread the cubes in an even layer on the prepared baking sheet.

continued

Bake until they are just starting to crisp and turn golden brown, 10 minutes. Top the croutons with the cheese and bake until the cheese has melted, about 5 minutes.

5 To serve, pour the soup into individual bowls and garnish with the croutons.

CHEESY CROUTON VARIATIONS Many different types of cheese will make delicious grilled-cheese croutons—just choose one that melts easily. Try soft cheeses like Brie, Camembert, or a fresh goat cheese for a creamy alternative.

planning ahead

When it comes to making a weekly meal lineup, I'm someone who thrives on having a plan in place. It's the best way to avoid the dreaded daily 5 p.m. question of what's for dinner tonight.

Here are some tips to help you plan ahead:

SET A SPECIFIC TIME EACH WEEK TO MENU PLAN. Determine when you will be home that week and how many nights you will be cooking. Use this time to flip through cookbooks or search your favorite web resources. Try a new recipe or two every week to keep things fresh and exciting.

GET EVERYONE INVOLVED. Asking your spouse, roommate, or kids what they would like to eat for the upcoming week is a great way to get the whole house involved. It's an invitation to participate, and kids especially like to get in on the action. If you have picky eaters, this may be the solution to getting them excited about what meals are coming up.

BE REALISTIC WITH YOUR COOKING AMBITIONS— PLAN NIGHTS OF EASY COOKING, TOO. Don't let yourself burn out in the kitchen by striving all the time. Some recipes in this book are made for last-minute, easy, or one-pot meals. See Fusilli Caesar Salad (page 85) and Chicken and Poblano Stew (page 124), both of which use rotisserie chicken, or the elegant Sweet Pea Soup (page 108), which is made entirely out of pantry ingredients. A stir-fry is another flexible dinner solution for when you want to get in and out of the kitchen fast (see page 128 for the best technique).

MAKE A MASTER SHOPPING LIST FOR THE WEEK. Once you've determined how often you'll be cooking and what the recipe lineup is, a master shopping list will help eliminate multiple trips to the grocery store. A quick scan of your pantry will also help avoid buying ingredients that you already have on hand.

VEGETABLE BARLEY SOUP

2 tablespoons unsalted butter

1 medium yellow onion, chopped

2 ribs celery, chopped

2 carrots, chopped

1 small yellow squash, chopped

2 teaspoons Italian seasoning

Kosher salt and cracked black pepper

6 cups vegetable broth or water

1 (16-ounce) can crushed tomatoes

½ cup ketchup

½ cup pearl barley

Ever since he was a kid, my younger brother, Cole, has loved this vegetarian soup, a family recipe that is one of his favorite things. This dish is a good example of the magic touch that my mom seems to have with vegetables—she never really had to "sneak" them in anywhere when we were kids. The abundance of vegetables and nuttiness from the barley make this soup hearty, yet not too heavy. While I'm usually a fan of fresh herbs, I think a slowly simmered soup or stew like this is the perfect place for dried herbs and spices from your pantry. To make life even easier, I like to keep a few seasoning blends on hand, such as herbes de Provence, Old Bay, and Italian seasoning (the perfect complement to the veggies and barley here).

SERVES **6 to 8** • PREP **15 minutes** • COOK **1 hour 20 minutes**

1 In a large soup pot set over medium heat, melt the butter. Add the onion, celery, carrots, squash, and Italian seasoning and season to taste with salt and pepper. Cook, stirring frequently, until the vegetables have softened and are fragrant, about 6 minutes. Add the broth, tomatoes, ketchup, and barley and bring the mixture to a boil. Reduce the heat to medium-low, cover, and cook for 30 minutes.

2 Uncover, stir, and cook until the flavors have a chance to fully develop, about 30 minutes longer. (The soup will keep in an airtight container in the refrigerator for up to 3 days.)

3 Season to taste with salt and pepper and serve hot.

BEAN AND HOMINY CHILI

SOUP

2 tablespoons
vegetable oil

2 medium onions, finely
chopped

1 poblano pepper,
chopped

3 garlic cloves, minced

3 tablespoons chili
powder

1 teaspoon ground cumin

1 teaspoon ground
coriander

1 teaspoon kosher
salt, plus more
as needed

¼ teaspoon cayenne
pepper (optional)

1 (14.5-ounce) can fire-
roasted whole tomatoes,
crushed by hand

1 (15.5-ounce) can white
hominy, drained and
rinsed

1 (15.5-ounce) can black
beans, drained and
rinsed

1 (15.5-ounce) can red
kidney beans, drained
and rinsed

Whether cooking a pot of chili for the big game or keeping up my family tradition of making it on Halloween night every year, I turn to this recipe, which is comforting and full of great memories. Though vegetarian, it's still hearty from black beans, kidney beans, and hominy—which I love for its chewy texture—and is ready to be garnished with anything you like. A few of my favorite Mexican ingredients, including poblano peppers, cumin, and coriander, round out the flavors. (If you wanted to make this solely from your pantry, consider substituting a 4-ounce can of green chiles for the poblano.) I like to serve this with buttery Sweet Cornbread (page 174), which pairs nicely with the slightly spicy flavors.

SERVES **4 to 6** • PREP **15 minutes** • COOK **1 hour**

1 In a large soup pot or Dutch oven set over medium-high heat, heat the oil. Add the onions and poblano and cook, stirring, until softened and beginning to brown, about 5 minutes. Add the garlic, chili powder, cumin, coriander, salt, and cayenne (if using). Cook, stirring constantly, until the spices are fragrant and toasted, 1 to 2 minutes. Add the tomatoes and bring to a simmer, scraping up any bits from the bottom of the pan. Add the hominy, black beans, kidney beans, and 4 cups water. Bring to a boil, reduce the heat to medium-low, cover, and simmer until thickened, about 45 minutes. Season to taste with salt.

2 To serve, ladle the chili into soup bowls and serve with bowls of the garnishes alongside, if desired.

½ medium red onion,
finely chopped

Sour cream

½ cup cilantro leaves,
chopped

¼ pound cheddar
cheese, shredded (1 cup)

Lime wedges

1 avocado, sliced

MEATY BEAN AND HOMINY CHILI For meat lovers, you could easily start off this recipe by browning 1 pound ground chuck or bison in an additional 1 tablespoon oil. Remove the meat from the pot and reserve. Proceed with the soup as directed, adding the browned meat back in when you add the beans.

season and taste

One of the fastest ways to transition from being a good home cook to a great one is to start tasting and seasoning your food every step of the way. Even highly calibrated recipes cannot account for your palate and preferences, or the strength of your pepper, for example. So these variables need to be addressed and adjusted by the cook. Proper use of ingredients as simple—but, in my opinion, underutilized—as salt and pepper makes all the difference in the world.

I always have a saltcellar filled with kosher salt and my trusty pepper grinder out on my counter so that it's easy to add a dash here and there. Tasting and then seasoning your food after each and every step of the cooking process will begin to build flavor that cannot be matched otherwise—meaning your dishes will likely require no salt and pepper once they actually hit the dinner table, the sign of a great home cook.

MAIN COURSES

5 Add the onion to the skillet, season with salt, and cook until translucent and softened, 1 to 2 minutes. Add the garlic and cook for 1 minute. Add the baguette cubes, potatoes, carrots, lemon wedges, and thyme; season with salt and pepper. Toss everything in the fat (add an additional glug of oil if the pan looks dry). Arrange the chicken thighs on top of the vegetable and crouton mixture.

6 Bake until the thighs are cooked through and reach 160°F on a thermometer inserted into the thickest part of a thigh, about 20 minutes.

7 To serve, divide the chicken and vegetables evenly among 4 plates or serve the dish family-style at the table.

PAN-ROASTING

Pan-roasting is a popular cooking method with restaurant chefs, but works wonders in a home kitchen as well. The technique is simple and straightforward, making use of both the stovetop and oven.

It's essential to use an ovenproof pan that will hold heat well; I really like using my cast-iron skillet (see page 159).

Use this technique to cook thick, small pieces of meat like steaks, pork chops, and bone-in chicken pieces, and meaty fish like salmon and mahi-mahi. Pan-searing first crisps up the outside and develops a ton of flavor through browning—plus sets you up for a delicious pan sauce later. Then, by finishing the food in the oven, you can cook the meat or fish evenly, leaving the interior super moist and juicy.

• Preheat the oven to moderately high heat (375° to 425°F).

• Heat a little bit of oil in a heavy ovenproof skillet over medium-high heat until very hot. Add the meat and sear on both sides until browned.

• Carefully transfer the pan to the oven, where the meat will finish roasting until cooked through.

• Remove the skillet from the oven and set the meat on a plate or cutting board to rest.

• Make a pan sauce (see page 146), if desired.

CHICKEN AND POBLANO
STEW

SERVES **4** • PREP **20 minutes** • COOK **45 minutes**

1 (3- to 4-pound) rotisserie chicken

1 poblano pepper

3 tablespoons vegetable oil

1 large yellow onion, chopped

4 garlic cloves, minced

1 tablespoon ground coriander

1½ teaspoons ground cumin

2 cups store-bought salsa verde

4 cups low-sodium chicken broth

Kosher salt and cracked black pepper

2 cups cooked long-grain white rice, for serving

Like everyone, I love one-pot recipes that are primarily based on pantry staples, and so this hearty stew is a regular in my kitchen. If it's been a long day, all I have to do is swing by the store and grab a rotisserie chicken and a poblano pepper; everything else is sitting in my pantry. Roasting the poblano is the only step that requires a little bit of work, but it sure pays off, contributing a deep smokiness and complex, not-too-hot chile flavor that can't be achieved otherwise. Serving the stew with rice really makes a filling, stand-alone meal, and a great way to sop up all of that delicious sauce!

1 Remove the meat from the chicken and shred it into 1-inch pieces; discard the skin and bones. Set aside about 1½ cups of the meat for the stew; reserve the remaining chicken for another use.

2 Roast the poblano over a flame until charred all over. (Alternatively, quarter the pepper, place the pieces skin side up on a baking sheet, and broil on the top rack until the skin has blistered and charred, 8 to 10 minutes.) Transfer the pepper (or pepper quarters) to a bowl, cover with plastic wrap, and let cool. When cool enough to handle, peel the poblano, discarding the stem and seeds if still whole. Chop the flesh.

3 In a large Dutch oven or saucepan set over medium heat, heat the oil. Add the onion and cook until translucent and fragrant, about 8 minutes. Add the garlic and roasted poblano and cook for 3 to 4 minutes. Add the coriander

GARNISHES (OPTIONAL)

1 red onion, finely chopped

1 lime, cut into wedges

½ cup Mexican crema or sour cream

Crushed tortilla chips

½ cup fresh cilantro leaves, chopped

1 avocado, cut into wedges

and cumin and cook until slightly darkened and fragrant, 2 to 3 minutes. Add the salsa verde and cook until it just comes to a boil, about 2 minutes. Add the chicken broth and return to a boil. Reduce the heat to medium and simmer for at least 10 minutes to allow the flavors to develop. Season to taste with salt and pepper. Add the shredded chicken and cook until heated through, 3 minutes.

4 To serve, divide the cooked rice among 4 bowls. Ladle the stew over the rice. Put the garnishes, if using, into serving bowls and serve alongside the stew.

wooden spoons and spring-loaded tongs

There is no such thing as having too many wooden spoons. I feel comfortable with one in my hand and so it's always the first tool I grab, passing up the silicone-coated tools and scrapers. Wooden spoons are great for everything—from scraping browned bits off the bottom of skillets (even nonstick) to stirring lemonade—and they don't conduct heat, even when propped up against the side of a saucepan.

Tongs are similarly important. I've got them in a variety of sizes and I use them almost every day. They wear many hats in my kitchen: flipping a steak or delicate piece of fish without piercing it, tossing a salad, reaching into boiling water to test pasta for doneness, or helping maneuver hot pans/lids/oven shelves when a dish towel is too far away.

Each of these essential tools act as an extension of your arm and make your work in the kitchen more efficient—I'd be lost without them.

STEAK AND PEPPER STIR-FRY

¼ cup rice vinegar

¼ cup low-sodium
soy sauce

1 teaspoon grated orange
zest

3 tablespoons sugar

1 teaspoon plus
1 tablespoon cornstarch

1¼ pounds flank steak,
thinly sliced against the
grain

Kosher salt and cracked
black pepper

2 tablespoons peanut oil

1 medium yellow onion,
thinly sliced

2 red bell peppers,
seeded and thinly sliced

2 garlic cloves, minced

2 teaspoons minced fresh
ginger

1 (10-ounce) package
rice noodles, cooked, or
2 cups cooked rice, for
serving

¼ cup cilantro leaves,
torn, for garnish

When I have zero brain power left after a long day, I default to stir-fry for dinner and always end up feeling satisfied that I pulled together a delicious meal with little effort. For a quick cooking method like stir-frying, I'm a huge fan of flavorful, chewy flank steak, sliced thin against the grain. The hint of orange in the sauce is a surprisingly successful match for the beef and peppers and complements the Asian flavor of the dish. I flip-flop when it comes to what to serve with this stir-fry: I like both rice or rice noodles.

1 In a small bowl or glass measuring cup, whisk together the vinegar, soy sauce, orange zest, sugar, and 1 teaspoon of the cornstarch.

2 Put the steak in a small bowl and sprinkle it with salt, pepper, and the remaining 1 tablespoon cornstarch. Toss to coat.

3 In a large skillet or wok set over high heat, heat the oil. Add the steak and stir-fry until the meat is almost cooked through and beginning to brown, about 2 minutes. Transfer the steak to a plate. Add the onion, bell peppers, garlic, and ginger to the pan and stir-fry until the vegetables are tender, about 5 minutes. Return the flank steak to the pan and cook for 1 minute longer.

4 Whisk the soy sauce mixture and add it to the skillet. Cook until the sauce thickens, 2 to 3 minutes.

5 Serve the stir-fry over rice noodles or rice and garnish with the cilantro.

PORK AND PINEAPPLE STIR-FRY Replace the steak with 1¼ pounds pork tenderloin, thinly sliced. Add ¾ cup chopped fresh pineapple to the vegetables.

MANDARIN CHINESE STIR-FRY Season the steak with 2 teaspoons Chinese 5-spice powder. Toss in ½ cup drained mandarin orange segments at the end.

STIR-FRYING

Stir-frying is one of the techniques that I rely on most when it comes to making a fast meal and using up odds and ends in the refrigerator. It's the ultimate kitchen-sink meal.

Here are some ways to make your stir-fry easy and delicious:

- Call me crazy, but I actually prefer working with a LARGE NONSTICK SKILLET instead of a wok when I'm cooking at home. I find that the flat surface area of the skillet browns the food better rather than the sloped surface of a wok, meaning you need one less pan to own and store.

- It will be even more important than usual to HAVE ALL OF YOUR INGREDIENTS PREPPED and ready to go because a stir-fry goes fast. Make sure your vegetables and meats or seafood are all cut into small, equal-size pieces for even cooking.

- The secret to a great stir-fry is HIGH HEAT. Too many home cooks are afraid to work with such intense heat, but it's essential for this cooking method. Make sure your pan is preheated and smoking hot before beginning.

- COOK IN STAGES. Rather than trying to cook everything perfectly at once, add small groups of ingredients at a time (hard veggies separately from soft veggies), stir-fry until tender, and remove from the pan and reserve. In fact, stir-fry your meat or seafood a minute or two shy of being cooked through. After everything has been cooked, toss it all in the pan together with your sauce ingredients to finish cooking and to bring the whole dish together. This avoids overcooking and helps maintain tenderness.

TORTELLINI

WITH SNAP PEAS AND LEMON-DILL CREAM

This weeknight dish is one of my husband's favorites, and I know that I can make it in about half an hour. I cook it so often that I always keep the ingredients on hand: rich filled pasta, Parmesan, pancetta—and fresh dill and lemon to add a light freshness to the creamy sauce. And by varying the ingredients in the sauce, I can create dishes that are just as tasty as this yet completely different, based on what I have on hand in my pantry.

SERVES **4 to 6** • PREP **10 minutes** • COOK **25 minutes**

1 pound refrigerated cheese tortellini

1 cup sugar snap peas, strings and ends removed, cut into thirds on an angle

1 tablespoon extra-virgin olive oil

3 ounces pancetta, cut into ¼-inch dice

1 shallot, finely chopped

¾ cup heavy cream

¼ cup low-sodium chicken broth

2 teaspoons finely chopped fresh dill, plus more for garnish

1 teaspoon grated lemon zest

⅓ cup grated Parmesan cheese

1 Bring a large pot of salted water to a boil. Add the tortellini and cook according to the package directions, adding the sugar snaps during the last 2 minutes of cooking. Drain and set aside.

2 In a large skillet set over medium-high heat, heat the oil. Add the pancetta and cook until crisp, 6 to 8 minutes. Using a slotted spoon, transfer the pancetta to a small bowl. Pour off all but 2 tablespoons of fat from the pan. Add the shallot and cook, stirring occasionally, until golden brown around the edges, about 2 minutes. Add the heavy cream, chicken broth, dill, and lemon zest. Bring to a boil, reduce the heat to medium, and simmer until the sauce has thickened and coats the back of a spoon, about 5 minutes. Add the tortellini, peas, and pancetta to the sauce and toss gently to coat.

3 To serve, divide the tortellini among 4 to 6 serving plates, and sprinkle with the Parmesan cheese. Garnish with dill.

TORTELLINI WITH TOMATO CREAM AND BASIL
Substitute haricots verts for the snap peas. Add a 14-ounce can of crushed San Marzano tomatoes to the pan after cooking the shallot. Substitute basil for the dill, and top with fresh cubed mozzarella instead of Parmesan.

GRILLED PORK CHOPS

WITH PEACH BBQ SAUCE

SERVES **4** • PREP **20 minutes** • COOK **20 minutes**

The contrasting flavors of the smoky, spicy rub and the sweet, fruity BBQ sauce are what make this recipe really special. Chipotle powder is worth seeking out for this rub, as it has just a bit of heat but a lot of boldness; the rest of the spices can be found in your spice cabinet. The sweet peach barbecue sauce easily comes together in a blender or food processor and serves two purposes: a glaze for the chops and a tangy sauce to serve on the side. If you don't have access to an outdoor grill, fire up a grill pan over high heat and sear until browned and cooked through; the addition of the smoked paprika and chipotle powder does a great job of imparting smoky flavors to the meat, so you don't end up missing out on the flavors achieved with an outdoor grill. (See page 157 for more on indoor grilling.)

PEACH BBQ SAUCE

4 cups peeled and sliced peaches or thawed frozen peaches

⅔ cup ketchup

⅔ cup apple cider vinegar

¼ cup low-sodium soy sauce

1 cup packed light brown sugar

2 garlic cloves, minced

2 teaspoons minced fresh ginger

1 **For the peach BBQ sauce:** In a food processor or blender, combine the peaches, ketchup, vinegar, soy sauce, brown sugar, garlic, and ginger and puree until smooth. Transfer to a saucepan and bring to a simmer over medium-high heat. Simmer until slightly reduced and thickened, about 10 minutes. Set aside ¼ cup for basting and reserve the remaining sauce for serving.

PORK CHOPS

Vegetable oil

2 teaspoons light brown sugar

2 teaspoons smoked paprika

2 teaspoons dry mustard

1 teaspoon garlic powder

1 teaspoon onion powder

1½ teaspoons kosher salt

1 teaspoon cracked black pepper

½ teaspoon chipotle powder

4 (¾-inch-thick) center-cut bone-in pork chops

2 **For the pork chops:** Preheat a grill or a grill pan to medium-high heat. Brush with vegetable oil to prevent sticking.

3 In a small bowl, combine the brown sugar, paprika, dry mustard, garlic powder, onion powder, salt, pepper, and chipotle powder. Season both sides of the pork chops generously with the spice rub, pressing to adhere. Put the pork chops on the grill and cook for 2 minutes per side. Brush the chops generously with the BBQ sauce reserved for basting and continue to grill until cooked through, about 1 more minute per side, brushing frequently with the sauce. Remove the chops from the grill and let rest for 5 minutes.

4 Serve the reserved BBQ sauce on the side.

PAN-ROASTED PORK CHOPS Another way I love to prepare pork chops at home is to pan-roast them (see page 143). This is a particularly good method if your chops are thicker than ¾ inch. Sear the chops in a hot cast-iron skillet for 2 minutes on each side, then baste with the BBQ sauce and transfer the skillet to a 400°F oven. Roast until the chops are cooked through, about 5 minutes. Serve with additional BBQ sauce on the side.

POT ROAST

WITH POTATOES AND ROOT VEGETABLES

SERVES **8** • PREP **10 minutes** • COOK **4 hours**

1 (4-pound) boneless chuck roast

Kosher salt and cracked black pepper

3 tablespoons vegetable oil

1 large yellow onion, chopped

1½ pounds small red potatoes, halved

4 large carrots, cut into 1-inch pieces (about 1½ cups)

3 parsnips, peeled and cut into 1-inch pieces (about 1 cup)

4 garlic cloves, minced

3 sprigs fresh thyme

1 cup dry red wine

2½ cups low-sodium beef broth

2 tablespoons Worcestershire sauce

1 tablespoon chopped fresh flat-leaf parsley, for garnish

When I think of pot roast, I think of Sundays at my grandma's house, where extended family would regularly gather to enjoy a meal together. This classic, hearty, and homey dish—the center of my grandmother's table—is a perfect one-pot "meat and potatoes" meal. The low-and-slow braise creates both tender meat and vegetables rich with flavor (see page 167 for more on braising). I like serving this alongside simple greens dressed in a tangy vinaigrette. The freshness of the greens balances the deep colors and flavors in this dish.

1 Preheat the oven to 350°F.

2 Using paper towels, pat the roast dry and season it liberally with salt and pepper. In a large Dutch oven set over medium heat, heat 2 tablespoons of the oil. Add the roast and brown it on all sides, 8 to 10 minutes. Transfer the roast to a cutting board or a large plate.

3 Add the remaining 1 tablespoon oil to the pot. Add the onion, potatoes, carrots, parsnips, garlic, and thyme, and season with salt and pepper. Cook until the vegetables start to brown, 5 to 10 minutes. Add ½ cup of the wine and cook, scraping up any bits from the bottom of the pot, until reduced by half, 3 to 5 minutes. Return the roast to the pot and add the beef broth and Worcestershire sauce. Bring the liquid to a simmer, cover with a tight-fitting lid, and put the pot in the oven.

continued

4 Roast the meat until fork-tender, flipping it once halfway through, about 3½ hours. Transfer the roast to a large cutting board, tent it with foil, and let it rest. Using a slotted spoon, transfer the vegetables to a serving platter. Put the Dutch oven back on the stovetop over medium-high heat. Add the remaining ½ cup wine, bring to a simmer, and cook until reduced by half, 5 to 10 minutes.

5 Strain the sauce and season to taste with salt and pepper. Shred the pot roast into big chunks and transfer to the platter with the vegetables. Sprinkle the vegetables and roast with the parsley. Reserve 1 cup of the sauce to pass when serving and pour the remainder over the vegetables and pot roast.

cutting boards

No kitchen should be without a large, heavy, solid-wood cutting board. A good-quality cutting board provides an excellent work surface for slicing and dicing. Get one that is large enough to push ingredients to the side and still have room to chop more (you'll eliminate the need for tons of prep bowls). Wood is certainly the kindest surface for the blades of your knives, helping you maintain a sharp edge as long as possible. A good maple or beech cutting board doesn't scar easily and is almost self-healing, especially when you take care of it—occasionally rub it with mineral oil to protect it from warping or staining. Bamboo cutting boards are another great option as they absorb less liquid than other wood boards and are made from a sustainable resource. However, they are a bit harder than a traditional cutting board, meaning that they are also a bit harder on your knives.

The only instances in which I pull out a plastic cutting board are to prevent any cross-contamination when I'm working with raw meat, poultry, or fish—and it must be a heavy-duty plastic. The flimsy ones simply won't do; they hurt your knives and can scar easily—meaning there's a possibility of plastic getting into your food—and should be kicked out of your kitchen.

SWEET POTATO–COCONUT CURRY

2 tablespoons vegetable oil

2 tablespoons curry powder

2 medium sweet potatoes (1 pound), peeled and cut into 1-inch cubes

1 large yellow onion, roughly chopped

2 garlic cloves, minced

1 tablespoon minced fresh ginger

½ serrano chile, minced

1 (14-ounce) can coconut milk

3 tablespoons light brown sugar

3 plum tomatoes, chopped (about 1 cup)

1 cup snow peas, trimmed

2 cups cooked jasmine rice, for serving

⅓ cup chopped salted peanuts, for garnish

¼ cup chopped fresh Thai basil or cilantro, for garnish

SERVES 4 • PREP 15 minutes • COOK 20 minutes

This simple curry dish comes together quickly and has a big payoff when it comes to flavor and presentation. Curry powder packs a punch in the spice department and it's a great secret weapon to keep on hand for a weeknight dinner when you want to throw together a dish that varies from your regular routine. This recipe has just the right balance of sweet and heat, and the sweet potatoes add so much flavor and texture that you don't notice the lack of any meat. (Just ask my husband!)

1 In a large skillet set over medium-high heat, heat the oil. Add the curry powder and toast until fragrant, about 1 minute. Add the sweet potatoes and onion and stir to coat with the curry oil. Cover and cook until the vegetables start to soften, about 3 minutes. Add the garlic, ginger, and chile and cook for 1 minute. Add the coconut milk and sugar, and stir, scraping up any bits from the bottom of the pan. Bring to a simmer, cover, and cook for 5 minutes. Add the tomatoes and snow peas and cook until the snow peas are crisp-tender, about 1 minute.

2 Serve the curry over the rice. Garnish with the peanuts and Thai basil.

CARNITAS TACOS WITH PICKLED RED ONIONS

SERVES **8** • PREP **25 minutes plus standing time** • COOK **3 hours**

PICKLED RED ONIONS

⅓ cup fresh lime juice

⅓ cup red wine vinegar

⅓ cup sugar

1 tablespoon kosher salt

1 jalapeño, seeded and cut into rings

½ medium red onion, thinly sliced

CARNITAS

1 (3-pound) boneless pork shoulder (butt), trimmed of excess fat

Juice of 4 limes

1 cup orange juice

4 garlic cloves, smashed

3 tablespoons chili powder

1 teaspoon ground coriander

1 teaspoon ground cumin

1 tablespoon kosher salt

16 (6-inch) corn tortillas, warmed

When it comes to carnitas, I take advice only from the best Tex-Mex cook I know, my friend Treva, born and raised in San Antonio, Texas. She rocked my world when she shared her mom's secrets to great carnitas: You first braise the pork in just enough orange juice to cover the meat; then you turn up the heat and let the liquid evaporate, until you're left with tiny tender pieces of generously seasoned pork crisping in their own rendered fat. (See page 167 for more on braising.) My tacos have never been the same since learning this Texan insider tip. I took the extra step to introduce a few other flavors like lime, garlic, and what I call the triple threat of Mexican spices: chili powder, coriander, and cumin. Served in warm tortillas and topped with proper fixin's—especially fresh-tasting, homemade pickled onions—carnitas will feed a crowd easily.

1 **For the pickled red onions:** In a small saucepan, combine the lime juice, vinegar, sugar, salt, and jalapeño. Bring to a simmer over medium-high heat, stirring occasionally until the sugar dissolves, about 2 minutes.

2 Place the onion slices in a bowl and pour the vinegar mixture over them. Cover with plastic wrap and let cool for about 20 minutes. Transfer to the refrigerator for at least 15 minutes and up to 2 days.

3 **For the carnitas:** Cut the pork shoulder into 1½- to 2-inch pieces and put them in a large Dutch oven or heavy pot. Add the lime juice, orange juice, garlic, chili powder,

continued

1 large avocado, chopped or sliced

¼ cup chopped fresh cilantro

½ cup shredded red cabbage

⅓ cup crumbled Cotija cheese

8 lime wedges

coriander, cumin, and salt. Add just enough water to cover the pork and bring the mixture to a boil. Reduce the heat to medium-low, cover, and cook for 30 minutes. Remove the lid and continue cooking at a gentle simmer for at least 1½ hours but no longer than 2 hours, stirring occasionally and taking care that there is still liquid in the pot.

4 Increase the heat to medium-high and cook, stirring, until all of the liquid has been absorbed or evaporated, about 10 minutes. Continue cooking, carefully turning the pork pieces, until they develop brown, crispy edges, about 5 minutes.

5 Serve the pork with the pickled onions, warmed tortillas, and, if desired, avocado, cilantro, cabbage, cheese, and lime wedges for squeezing.

QUICK-PICKLE GARNISHES You can use the method for the quick-pickled onions for peppers, radishes, or even cabbage. Just slice the vegetables thinly and taste them as they sit in the pickling solution—tougher vegetables like cabbage may need a bit more time in the vinegar mixture. (See page 57 for more information on quick-pickling.)

POACHED SALMON

WITH ORANGE-GINGER SAUCE

SERVES **4** • PREP **20 minutes** • COOK **10 minutes**

ORANGE-GINGER SAUCE

½ cup sour cream

¼ cup mayonnaise

2 tablespoons orange juice

2 tablespoons unseasoned rice vinegar

2 teaspoons whole-grain mustard

2 teaspoons minced fresh ginger

Grated zest of ½ orange

Kosher salt and cracked black pepper

POACHED SALMON

Juice of ½ orange

1 (2-inch) piece ginger, cut into rounds

4 (6-ounce) skinless center-cut salmon fillets (about 1 inch thick)

Kosher salt and cracked black pepper

A beautifully poached piece of fish is fresh, light, and clean tasting, making it a perfect meal to enjoy in the spring or summer months. Cooking salmon ever so gently in simmering liquid until just the center is translucent results in a flaky piece of fish that has been infused with flavor in no time. I like serving it with this creamy, no-cook orange-ginger sauce that incorporates the same flavors as the poaching liquid. Serving it over a bed of sautéed baby bok choy or spinach is a gorgeous way to complete the dish. Any leftovers would be fantastic flaked into a salad or even formed into salmon patties and fried.

1 **For the orange-ginger sauce:** In a small bowl, whisk together the sour cream, mayonnaise, orange juice, vinegar, mustard, ginger, and orange zest. Season to taste with salt and pepper. Set aside at room temperature just until the salmon is finished cooking to allow the flavors to develop.

2 **For the salmon:** In a large deep skillet, combine the orange juice, ginger, and 1 quart water. Cover and bring the poaching liquid to a boil over medium-high heat. Season the salmon fillets with salt and pepper. Reduce the heat to medium, then gently slide the salmon fillets into the poaching liquid. Cover the pan and cook until the salmon is just opaque, 6 to 8 minutes.

3 Transfer the salmon to 4 serving plates. Spoon the sauce over the top and serve.

PAN-SEARED SCALLOPS

WITH CHIMICHURRI

If you're looking for a refined dinner that comes together in mere minutes, this is the recipe for you. Scallops are best served when they are quickly seared, which develops a golden brown crust on each side. The result is a rich buttery flavor with great texture. I particularly love serving them with a bright, herby chimichurri, a delicious sauce hailing from South America, where it is so popular it's eaten with everything from grilled meats to leftovers from the refrigerator. It's incredibly easy to make and the ingredients can be found any time of year.

CHIMICHURRI

⅓ cup extra-virgin olive oil

2 tablespoons red wine vinegar

2 tablespoons fresh lime juice

3 garlic cloves

¾ cup fresh flat-leaf parsley leaves

¾ teaspoon kosher salt, plus more as needed

½ teaspoon red pepper flakes

SCALLOPS

2 tablespoons vegetable oil

16 large sea scallops, feet removed

Kosher salt and cracked black pepper

2 tablespoons unsalted butter

1 **For the chimichurri:** In a food processor or blender, combine the olive oil, vinegar, lime juice, garlic, parsley, salt, red pepper flakes, and 2 tablespoons water and puree until smooth. Taste and season with additional salt, if necessary. (The chimichurri can be made up to 4 hours in advance. Cover and chill until ready to use.)

2 **For the scallops:** In a large 12-inch cast-iron skillet set over medium-high heat, heat the vegetable oil. Dry the scallops well with paper towels and liberally season each side with salt and pepper. Put the scallops in the hot pan and cook until the bottoms start to brown around the edges, about 2 minutes. Add the butter to the pan to help them caramelize (don't add earlier or it could burn). Once the butter melts, flip the scallops and cook until golden brown on the second side and just cooked through, 2 to 3 minutes.

3 Divide the scallops among 4 serving plates, drizzle with chimichurri sauce, and serve.

CHICKEN PICCATA

SERVES **4** • PREP **15 minutes** • COOK **25 minutes**

2 boneless, skinless chicken breasts

Kosher salt and cracked black pepper

½ cup all-purpose flour

4 tablespoons extra-virgin olive oil

½ cup (1 stick) unsalted butter

Grated zest and juice of 1 lemon

1 cup low-sodium chicken broth

2 tablespoons capers, rinsed

1 tablespoon chopped fresh flat-leaf parsley

Chicken breasts may just be the foundation of the most popular dinners in America. Unfortunately, when not cooked correctly, they can be dry and flavorless. Fortunately, this sad fate is easily avoided by slicing each breast horizontally into two thinner, more uniform pieces. The chicken cutlets cook much more quickly, ensuring a juicier result. The technique of dredging and pan-frying creates both a light, crispy crust on the chicken and a lot of delicious browned bits on the bottom of the pan. The simple pan sauce of lemon juice, briny capers, and fresh parsley makes a perfect bright counterpoint to the chicken. I love serving this chicken piccata over a bed of angel hair pasta tossed with olive oil and chopped fresh garden tomatoes—the pairing is easy enough to be a weeknight staple.

1 Put one of the chicken breasts on a cutting board. Keeping your knife blade parallel to the cutting board, cut into the thickest part of the chicken breast. Slice horizontally all the way through the chicken breast to make two thinner pieces that are about ½ inch thick. Repeat with the other chicken breast. Season the cutlets liberally with salt and pepper. Place the flour in a shallow dish and dredge the chicken in the flour, shaking off any excess.

2 In a large skillet set over medium-high heat, heat 2 tablespoons of the oil and 2 tablespoons of the butter. Put 2 chicken cutlets in the skillet and cook until golden brown on one side, 3 to 5 minutes. Flip the chicken and cook until cooked through, about 1 minute longer.

Transfer the chicken to a plate and cover with foil to keep warm. Pour off the remaining oil and butter and wipe out the pan. Add the remaining 2 tablespoons oil and 2 tablespoons of the butter to the skillet and repeat the same steps for the 2 remaining chicken cutlets. Keep all the cooked cutlets under the foil.

3   Make a pan sauce by adding the lemon zest and juice, broth, and capers to the butter and oil in the skillet. Bring to a boil and, using a wooden spoon, scrape up any browned bits from the bottom of the pan (those bits add a lot of flavor). Cook until reduced by half, 3 to 5 minutes. Remove the skillet from the heat and whisk in the remaining 4 tablespoons butter. Season to taste with salt and pepper. Return the chicken to the pan and turn to coat it with the sauce.

4   To serve, put a chicken cutlet on each of 4 serving plates. Spoon the sauce over the chicken and garnish with the parsley.

CHICKEN PICCATA WITH PESTO Stir 1 tablespoon prepared pesto into the pan sauce. Substitute pine nuts for the capers, if desired.

MAKING PAN SAUCES

I've always been a firm believer that a simple pan sauce can make a good meal taste great. It's almost criminal not to take advantage of all the flavorful caramelized bits from the bottom of the pan when you sear a piece of meat. The method is basic and flexible, and the flavors developed are rich and refined. It's one of the most valuable skills I learned in culinary school—and the one that is perhaps the easiest to apply to the home kitchen. Once you get in the habit of whipping up these quick sauces, you'll never serve a meal without one.

- Pan-sear meat in a heavy skillet or pan. When cooked to your desired doneness, remove the meat from the pan and let it rest.

- Reduce the heat slightly and add aromatics like chopped onion, shallot, or garlic to the rendered fat in the pan, sautéing just until they begin to caramelize.

- Add liquid—such as wine, broth, or stock—to deglaze the pan, which means to scrape up the browned bits on the bottom of the pan (with a wooden spoon), using the liquid to help dissolve them. Now you can add additional flavorings or embellishments—like mustard, capers, or cream—if you like. Increase the heat and bring to a boil. Simmer to reduce until the sauce thickens enough to coat the back of a wooden spoon.

- Remove the pan from the heat and swirl in a pat or two of butter and some chopped fresh herbs, if desired.

- Season to taste with salt and pepper.

MOROCCAN-SPICED ROAST CHICKEN

WITH CREAMY CILANTRO SAUCE

SERVES 4 · **PREP 20 minutes** · **COOK 1 hour 30 minutes**

The first dish my mom taught me to make was a roast chicken, and I've been making variations of that classic ever since. This recipe is simple enough to prepare for an everyday meal and reliable enough to be a standby for special occasions like having the in-laws over or inviting your boss to dinner. The potatoes roast along with the chicken, resulting in an automatic side dish—though Israeli couscous is a delicious accompaniment as well. This particular version of roast chicken has fantastic flavor thanks to essential pantry spices, which provide great dimension. The cool yogurt-cilantro sauce is finger-licking good. I like this flavor line-up so much that I use the same spice combination and creamy sauce with pork tenderloin that I throw on the grill—when I don't want to heat up the kitchen.

CHICKEN

1 (5-pound) roasting chicken

Kosher salt and cracked black pepper

2 pounds small red potatoes, halved

6 tablespoons unsalted butter, at room temperature

1 teaspoon ground cinnamon

1 teaspoon ground coriander

1 teaspoon ground cumin

1 teaspoon paprika

1 lemon, halved

1 yellow onion, quartered

4 garlic cloves, smashed

1 **For the chicken:** Preheat the oven to 425°F.

2 Pat the chicken dry. Season the cavity of the chicken generously with salt and pepper. Put the chicken in the center of a roasting pan, breast side up, and surround it with the potatoes.

3 In a small bowl, combine the butter, cinnamon, coriander, cumin, paprika, and 1 teaspoon kosher salt. Spread 2 tablespoons of the spiced butter underneath the skin on the breast of the chicken, distributing it evenly. Spread the remaining butter over the entire surface of the chicken. Squeeze half of the lemon over the chicken. Stuff the remaining lemon half, the onion quarters, and garlic in the cavity. Tie the legs with kitchen string.

continued

1 cup (8 ounces) Greek yogurt

1 tablespoon extra-virgin olive oil

1 tablespoon fresh lemon juice

1 teaspoon Sriracha sauce

1 garlic clove, grated

1 tablespoon chopped fresh cilantro

Kosher salt and cracked black pepper

4 Roast until the chicken reaches 165°F on a thermometer inserted in the thickest part of the thigh, 1 to 1½ hours. Let the chicken stand for 10 minutes before carving.

5 **For the sauce:** Meanwhile, in a small bowl, whisk together the yogurt, oil, lemon juice, Sriracha, garlic, and cilantro. Season to taste with salt and pepper.

6 Serve the chicken with the potatoes and the creamy cilantro sauce on the side.

all-purpose digital thermometer

Having a no-frills, reliable thermometer in the kitchen is essential. It's your best friend when it comes to cooking meat properly, as you can easily check internal cooking temperatures without cutting deeply into the meat. It can make the difference between a dish that is perfectly cooked and a dish that is over- or underdone. In my opinion, the simpler the thermometer, the better.

Unwieldy thermometers with too many functions are confusing and may be difficult to use when you need a temperature reading right away. A basic, affordable digital thermometer will give you a reading for everything from a roast to cheesecake and should have a place in every home kitchen.

HERB-BUTTER ROASTED TURKEY

SERVES **8 to 10** • PREP **15 minutes plus standing time** • COOK **2 hours 30 minutes**

1 cup (2 sticks) unsalted butter, at room temperature

2 teaspoons chopped fresh sage plus ½ cup fresh sage leaves, torn

2 teaspoons chopped plus ½ bunch fresh thyme

2 teaspoons chopped plus ½ bunch fresh rosemary

1 (10- to 12-pound) whole turkey (neck, giblets, and liver removed)

Kosher salt and cracked black pepper

1 medium yellow onion, quartered

6 garlic cloves, smashed

For some reason, cooking a Thanksgiving turkey seems to win the award for the most intimidating experience in the kitchen. I know seasoned home cooks who still get nervous when they are in charge of the bird for the holiday. This recipe is as easy as turkey gets, and I always get fantastic results. I particularly like the simple ingredient list—butter, fresh herbs, garlic, salt, and pepper. The same ingredients work when cooking a single turkey breast instead of the whole bird—something I sometimes do over the weekend for delicious sandwiches and leftovers throughout the week.

1 Preheat the oven to 350°F.

2 In a small bowl, combine 1 stick of the butter and the chopped sage, thyme, and rosemary. Cube the remaining stick of butter and set aside.

3 Put the turkey on V-shaped rack in a large roasting pan. Pat the turkey dry. Working carefully so that you don't tear the skin, smear the herb butter evenly underneath the skin of the bird. Season the outside and inside the cavity liberally with salt and pepper. Loosely fill the cavity with the cubed butter, onion, garlic, torn sage, and the thyme and rosemary bunches. Tie the legs together with kitchen string and tuck the wings under the turkey.

4 Roast the turkey until the juices run clear and the turkey reaches 165°F on a thermometer inserted into the thickest part of the thigh, about 2½ hours. Transfer to a cutting board or platter, tent with foil, and let stand for 20 minutes before carving. (For pan gravy tips, see page 146.)

ROASTING

Roasting is as simple as drizzling meat, fish, or vegetables with a little oil, seasoning with salt and pepper (and other herbs or spices, if you like), and then letting the oven do all of the work. A dry, high-heat method of cooking, roasting seems to bring out the best in whatever you are cooking as it concentrates flavor and creates a caramelized crust. It's one of the easiest and most approachable cooking techniques out there.

YOU'LL NEED

- **A LARGE ROASTING PAN** that is about 2 inches deep is a great investment. Look for a heavy pan with handles that you can transfer from the oven to the stovetop to deglaze those valuable pan drippings. For smaller items like fruits and vegetables, a rimmed baking sheet works great.

- A digital **MEAT THERMOMETER** takes out the guesswork when roasting meats to their appropriate temperatures.

- **A METAL ROASTING RACK** is often helpful for roasting meat, to both help it cook evenly and achieve maximum browning by allowing the air to circulate. You can also create a rack out of a single layer of vegetables that the meat can rest on top of (carrots and celery are favorites, as they also add great flavor to the pan drippings).

INGREDIENTS BEST SUITED FOR ROASTING

- Roasting is an excellent method for large, tender cuts of beef (rib roast, filet), pork (tenderloins), lamb (bone-in or boneless leg of lamb), poultry (whole chickens, bone-in chicken pieces, turkey), and fish.

- When selecting vegetables, consider sturdy roots like potatoes, carrots, beets, and parsnips, as well as harder, crunchy vegetables like broccoli, cauliflower, Brussels sprouts, and asparagus.

- Choose firm fruits like apples, pears, or stone fruits. Tomatoes are also fantastic roasted—eat them as is, or grind them up for sauces. Simple roasted fruit, caramelized and warm from the oven, served alongside ice cream, is one of my favorite desserts.

OVEN-BAKED
RIBS
WITH TANGY BBQ SAUCE

RIBS

¼ cup packed dark brown sugar

¼ cup smoked paprika

2 tablespoons chili powder

2 tablespoons kosher salt

2 teaspoons garlic powder

1½ teaspoons cayenne pepper

1½ teaspoons ground cumin

1½ teaspoons dry mustard

1½ teaspoons celery salt

2 (4- to 5-pound) racks pork spareribs

TANGY BBQ SAUCE

1 (15-ounce) can tomato puree

1 cup honey

½ cup apple cider vinegar

2 tablespoons Worcestershire sauce

4 garlic cloves, grated

SERVES 6 to 8 • PREP 25 minutes • COOK 3 hours

Utilizing both your oven and a grill or grill pan to cook ribs results in fall-off-the-bone-tender meat and a crispy, charred exterior with a super-smoky flavor. The smoked paprika in the rub, a sweet and savory combo, adds another delicious layer of smokiness. The dark brown sugar is a good backdrop for the cayenne pepper and other spices. I always make extra rub and keep it in a tightly closed container—this way I have it on hand to use for another round of ribs or any other time the need for BBQ strikes.

1 **For the ribs:** Preheat the oven to 275°F. Prepare a baking sheet by placing a sheet of foil that's about twice the size of the baking sheet on top.

2 In a small bowl, combine the brown sugar, paprika, chili powder, salt, garlic powder, cayenne pepper, cumin, dry mustard, and celery salt. Set aside 1 tablespoon of the spice rub.

3 Put the ribs on the prepared baking sheet. Generously sprinkle the ribs on both sides with the remaining spice rub. Put the ribs meat side down, fold the foil over the ribs, and seal the edges to make a packet. Bake the ribs until they are pliable but not falling apart and the meat pulls away from the bone, 2 to 2½ hours. Carefully pour off ½ cup of the accumulated juices into a bowl and reserve. Keep the ribs wrapped in the foil to keep warm.

continued

4 **For the BBQ sauce:** In a small saucepan set over medium-high heat, combine the tomato puree, honey, vinegar, Worcestershire sauce, garlic, and reserved 1 tablespoon spice rub. Add the reserved cooking juices and bring the mixture to a boil. Reduce the heat to medium and simmer until the sauce thickens and coats the back of a spoon, about 10 minutes.

5 Preheat a grill or grill pan over high heat.

6 Slather the ribs with the BBQ sauce and put them on the grill or grill pan. Cook, basting them with the sauce and turning until they char, about 5 minutes. (If you don't have a grill or grill pan, you can slather them with sauce and stick them under the broiler to char.)

7 Serve the ribs with extra BBQ sauce on the side.

INDOOR GRILLING

When I moved to New York City I was heartbroken that I had to break up with outdoor grilling. So I made it my mission to make indoor grilling just as delicious. With minimal equipment and a couple of clever ingredients, your indoor-grilled dishes can mimic some of those flavors you associate only with the great outdoors.

TOOLS/EQUIPMENT

- Invest in a cast-iron grill pan that can get smokin' hot. This will give you both the grill marks and the hard-seared flavor that everyone loves about grilling. The more you use your cast-iron grill pan for indoor grilling, the better it will get, as it improves with every use (see page 159).

- Skewers can be helpful if you are grilling small veggies or pieces of meat. I like the flat ones the most, as they make it easier to flip the food. You can find disposable wooden or reusable metal ones—I don't have a preference. (But do remember to soak wooden ones in water for at least 30 minutes before skewering, so they won't catch fire in the pan.)

- A good vent or fan above your stove will keep your kitchen cool and smoke free even when grilling inside—this is the time to use it!

INGREDIENTS

- Incorporating smoked paprika, chipotle powder, or bacon can give you some of the authentic smoky flavors you're after.

- A little natural liquid smoke (used sparingly) can give your food that grill-kissed taste; it is made from burned mesquite and applewood and can usually be found in the grocery store right next to the BBQ sauces.

PAN-SEARED SPANISH STEAKS

2 (16-ounce) rib-eye steaks (about 1 inch thick), at room temperature

Canola oil

Kosher salt and cracked black pepper

2 shallots, thinly sliced

1 garlic clove, minced

½ cup low-sodium beef broth

2 tablespoons Worcestershire sauce

2 tablespoons sherry vinegar

2 tablespoons unsalted butter

¼ cup sliced Spanish olives (optional)

1 tablespoon chopped fresh chives

SERVES 4 • PREP 10 minutes • COOK 20 minutes

When we were newlyweds, my husband was convinced that steak was only a "restaurant meal." It didn't require much to change his mind beyond my searing two good steaks and whipping up a pan sauce with garlic and butter. Served alongside creamy smashed potatoes, this meal was one that scored me major points. One of the greatest things about making steak at home is that it's actually fast and easy. Here I give rib-eyes a Spanish flair by adding sherry vinegar and olives to the sauce. The key is using tried-and-true essential techniques (like dry, room-temperature meat and a very hot pan) and purchasing high-quality ingredients—develop a relationship with your local butcher if you haven't already.

1 Heat a 12-inch cast-iron skillet over high heat until very hot, about 3 minutes.

2 Thoroughly pat the steaks dry with a paper towel. Lightly coat each side of the steaks with oil and sprinkle generously with salt and pepper. Add 1 to 2 tablespoons of oil to the pan (this helps create a great crust on the steaks) and add the steaks. (Do not crowd them; if you cannot leave room between each steak, use 2 pans or cook the steaks in batches.) Without moving them, cook the steaks for 3 minutes. Using tongs, flip the steaks and cook another 1 minute for rare, 2 minutes for medium-rare, or 4 minutes for medium. Transfer the steaks to a plate and cover loosely with foil. Let the steaks rest for at least 5 minutes before slicing them.

3 Add a glug of oil to the skillet. Add the shallots and garlic and cook until fragrant and just beginning to brown, 3 to

5 minutes. Add the beef broth, Worcestershire sauce, and vinegar and bring to a boil. Cook until reduced by half, 3 to 5 minutes. Turn off the heat and whisk in the butter. Stir in the olives (if using).

4 Divide the sliced steaks among 4 plates, spoon the sauce over the top, sprinkle with the chives, and serve.

cast-iron skillet

If I were stranded on a desert island and could have only one kitchen item with me, it would be my cast-iron skillet. It actually gets better with age and will last a lifetime, or more, thanks to its strong and sturdy structure. (I'm the proud recipient of my grandma's cast-iron skillet.) The intense temperatures that can be achieved with cast iron guarantee beautifully seared meat. It's also the best tool for pan-roasting (see page 123) as it can go from stove to oven and back again. It can also be used as a baking dish for cobblers and quick breads, a roasting pan, even a weight for pressed sandwiches. You might think that a tool this versatile would be expensive, but that's not the case. A new, large cast-iron skillet won't cost you more than $25 to $30 and will be worth every penny.

One important thing to note: Never put a cast-iron skillet in the dishwasher, and bypass soap entirely. To properly clean your skillet, keep these tips in mind:

• Clean the skillet immediately after use, ideally while still warm.

• Wash the skillet by hand using hot water and a stiff brush or sponge. Avoid steel wool as it may strip the surface, and never soak the pan in water or it may rust.

• To remove stuck-on food, sprinkle kosher salt on the surface and scrub.

• After cleaning, return the skillet to the stove over low heat to dry it out completely, or thoroughly dry with a towel.

To season or re-season a traditional cast-iron skillet: Generously coat the skillet with vegetable oil, bake in a 350°F oven for about 1 hour, and let cool. Using paper towels, wipe the skillet dry. The pan is now ready to use. Each time you heat oil in the skillet, you will reinforce the nonstick coating. Any time you notice rust developing or the surface needs a nonstick refresher, simply repeat the seasoning process.

COD
EN PAPILLOTE
WITH TOMATOES, OLIVES, AND OREGANO

Cooking en papillote—meaning, in a paper envelope—is a simple method that infuses the main event with the flavors of whatever you include: fresh herbs, broths, or other seasonings. Ingredients steam quickly but gently so it's particularly good for delicate foods like white flaky fish—a blank canvas for building flavor. And of course there's the satisfaction of breaking open the packet after baking and being overtaken by the tantalizing smells steaming out the top—it turns an easy-to-assemble meal into a bona fide experience.

Grated zest and juice of 1 lemon

2 garlic cloves, minced

2 tablespoons dry white wine

2 tablespoons red wine vinegar

2 plum tomatoes, roughly chopped

½ cup mixed olives, pitted and chopped

1 shallot, thinly sliced (about ¼ cup)

4 sprigs fresh oregano

4 (6-ounce) cod fillets, about 1½ inches thick

Kosher salt and cracked black pepper

Extra-virgin olive oil, for brushing

1½ tablespoons chopped fresh flat-leaf parsley, for garnish

1 Preheat the oven to 425°F. Fold 4 (16 × 12-inch) rectangles of parchment paper in half crosswise. Unfold and divide the parchment pieces between 2 baking sheets.

2 In a small bowl, combine the lemon zest and juice, garlic, white wine, and vinegar.

3 Evenly divide the tomatoes, olives, shallot, and oregano sprigs among the parchment pieces, putting everything on one half of each piece to make a bed for the fish. Sprinkle each with 1 tablespoon of the lemon juice mixture. Put a cod fillet on top of each pile of vegetables and season to taste with salt and pepper. Sprinkle the fish with another tablespoon of the lemon juice mixture.

4 Fold the top half of the parchment over the fish, closing the paper packet like a book. Starting at one corner, by the packet's spine, make a series of small overlapping folds along the open edges to seal the packet, tucking the final fold underneath the packet so that it does not unfurl. Brush the outside of each packet with olive oil. Bake until the parchment paper puffs up, 8 to 10 minutes.

5 Transfer the parchment packets to 4 serving plates. Carefully cut the packets open, being sure to avoid the hot steam, and remove the oregano sprigs. Garnish with the parsley and serve.

TUNA NOODLE CASSEROLE

6 tablespoons unsalted butter

1 large yellow onion, finely chopped

Kosher salt and cracked black pepper

8 ounces white mushrooms, sliced (about 5 cups)

¼ cup dry sherry

2 teaspoons low-sodium soy sauce

¼ cup all-purpose flour

2 cups low-sodium chicken broth

1 cup whole milk

1 tablespoon fresh lemon juice

2 (5-ounce) cans water-packed solid white tuna, drained

8 ounces dried egg noodles (about 3 cups)

1 cup frozen petite peas, thawed

½ pound cheddar cheese, grated (2 cups)

¾ cup panko bread crumbs

Tuna noodle casserole is definitely a retro recipe—something from the past that you either hate to admit that you love, or that maybe you just hate. This homemade version—which eliminates the canned cream of mushroom soup and one-dimensional mushy texture—will make just about anybody a believer. It's crucial to purchase good canned tuna and old-fashioned egg noodles. The mild tuna flavor balances perfectly with the sautéed mushrooms, sweet peas, and indulgent cream sauce. And the crunchy topping of cheese and crispy crumbs is always what everyone clamors for. If you're still not convinced, this casserole would be just as delicious made with shredded chicken or turkey instead of tuna—a great way to use up leftover meat. For a really refined touch, bake and serve the casserole in individual ramekins.

SERVES 6 to 8 • **PREP 20 minutes** • **COOK 55 minutes**

1 Preheat the oven to 375°F. Butter a shallow 2-quart baking dish.

2 In a large heavy skillet set over medium-high heat, melt 1 tablespoon of the butter. Add the onion and cook, stirring, until translucent and fragrant, about 3 minutes. Season with salt and pepper. Add the mushrooms and cook, stirring occasionally, for 2 minutes. Add the sherry and soy sauce and cook until most of the liquid has evaporated, about 5 minutes. Remove the pan from the heat.

3 In a large heavy saucepan set over medium-low heat, melt 4 tablespoons of the butter. Add the flour and cook, whisking constantly, until the roux cooks and bubbles a bit, about 2 minutes (make sure it doesn't brown). While whisking constantly, slowly add the chicken broth. Bring to a boil. Whisk in the milk, reduce the heat to medium, and cook until thickened, about 5 minutes. Add the mushroom mixture, lemon juice, and tuna to the pan and stir just to combine. Season to taste with salt and pepper. Remove the pan from the heat.

4 Bring a large pot of salted water to a boil. Add the noodles and cook for 2 minutes. Add the peas and cook for 1 more minute. Drain the noodles and peas and return them to the pot. Add the sauce, stirring gently to coat the noodles. Transfer the mixture to the prepared baking dish.

5 In a small saucepan, melt the remaining 1 tablespoon butter. In a small bowl, combine the cheese and bread crumbs. Drizzle in the melted butter and toss. Sprinkle the mixture evenly over the top of the casserole. Bake until the topping is crisp and the sauce is bubbling, 20 to 25 minutes. Let cool slightly before serving.

SIDES

BUTTER-BRAISED CABBAGE

WITH BACON

SERVES **4** · PREP **15 minutes** · COOK **55 minutes**

4 slices thick-cut bacon
(4 ounces), chopped

6 tablespoons (¾ stick)
unsalted butter

1 large yellow onion,
thinly sliced

1 cup dry white wine

¼ cup apple cider
vinegar

½ head red cabbage,
thinly sliced

Kosher salt and cracked
black pepper

You know that you cannot go wrong with a side dish when it includes both butter and bacon! This is the most delicious cabbage dish known to man. The salty and smoky flavors in the bacon are absorbed into the cabbage, and the butter creates a silky sauce. The apple cider vinegar flavor is tangy and sweet and a nice counterpoint to such a rich combo. Braising cabbage mellows it completely and the slow, relaxed cooking lets you turn to the other parts of the meal. I like using red cabbage because of the bright color, but green cabbage would work just as well.

1 In a large saucepan set over medium-high heat, cook the bacon, stirring occasionally, until crisp, about 12 minutes. Using a slotted spoon, transfer the crisped bacon to a paper towel–lined plate and set aside.

2 Add the butter to the bacon drippings. Add the onion and cook until fragrant and translucent, 3 to 5 minutes. Add the wine, vinegar, and cabbage. Cover, reduce the heat to medium, and cook until the cabbage has softened and absorbed most of the liquid, about 30 minutes.

3 Uncover and cook until all the liquid has evaporated, 3 to 5 minutes. Stir in the crisped bacon, season with salt and pepper, and serve.

BRAISING

I invested in a good Dutch oven right after I was married and when the big heavy pot arrived I felt like we had just gained a beloved new member of the family. That fall and winter I braised anything that could be braised and fell in love with this simple, satisfying cooking method that yields such deep flavors. While braising is not necessarily "quick," the wonderful aromas that will fill your home after hours of sumptuous—largely unattended—cooking will be worth it.

INGREDIENTS BEST SUITED FOR BRAISING

- Use tougher, less expensive cuts of beef like chuck, brisket, rump roast, and round. When it comes to poultry and pork, use bone-in chicken pieces, a blade roast, thick pork chops, or "country-style" ribs. Any cubed stew meat is also a great candidate for braising. The process makes these tough cuts taste like a million bucks and cut like butter.

- Sturdy leafy vegetables (like cabbage and collards) and hard vegetables (like parsnips, rutabagas, and beets) become soft, silky, and permeated with flavor.

GETTING STARTED

- Brown your meat and/or vegetables in a Dutch oven on top of the stove.

- Pour the liquid of your choice (wine, stock, water) over the meat and/or vegetables, until it is about one-third of the way up the side of the ingredients.

- Cover and cook over low heat on top of the stove or in a 300°F oven for an extended period of time (we're talking hours, not minutes). A tight lid is essential to trap all the flavor and allow the moisture to stay locked in.

RAPID ROLLS

MAKES **2** • PREP **10 minutes plus rising time** • COOK **25 minutes**

3 (.25-ounce) packets active dry yeast

1¾ cups warm water (105° to 115°F)

½ cup honey

½ cup (1 stick) unsalted butter, melted, plus more for brushing

2 large eggs, beaten

2 teaspoons kosher salt, plus more for sprinkling

6 cups all-purpose flour, plus more as needed

The process of working with yeast dough, the comforting smells that drift from the oven, and the unmatched taste and texture of homemade bread are enough to make me want to run home and bake a loaf immediately. (See page 41 for more on working with yeast dough.) And with this super-fast recipe, I always can—even when I haven't planned ahead and have only an hour until dinner. In fact, because of the ease of this recipe, my sister-in-law Betsy, a busy mom to six darling kids, makes fresh bread for her family on a regular basis—lucky ducks!

1 Preheat the oven to 400°F.

2 In the bowl of a stand mixer fitted with the paddle attachment, combine the yeast and warm water. Let stand for 5 minutes until the yeast is bubbly and looks creamy. Turn the mixer on low speed and add the honey. Add the melted butter, eggs, and salt. Slowly add the flour, 1 cup at a time, until it is fully incorporated and the dough pulls away from the sides of the bowl, about 3 minutes. Add more flour if the dough is too sticky. Turn the dough out onto a floured work surface.

3 Divide the dough evenly into 24 pieces and roll them into balls. Space 12 rolls about 2 inches apart in a large (12-inch) cast-iron skillet or a 9 × 13-inch baking dish. Repeat with the remaining dough balls in another skillet or baking dish. Keep covered with a clean towel in a warm place and let the rolls rise until doubled in size, about 20 minutes.

continued

4 Brush the rolls with melted butter. Bake until the tops are golden brown, about 25 minutes. Remove the pans from the oven. Brush the rolls with more melted butter and sprinkle with a pinch of salt. Serve warm. (Store leftovers in an airtight container at room temperature for up to 3 days.)

SAUTÉED SPINACH WITH FETA

3 tablespoons unsalted butter

1 tablespoon extra-virgin olive oil

1 large shallot, finely chopped

1 garlic clove, minced

1/8 teaspoon freshly grated nutmeg

Kosher salt and cracked black pepper

1 pound baby spinach

1/4 cup crumbled feta cheese

It's always nice to have a few quick sautéed greens recipes in your back pocket to pair with easy meals. Whether you fancy Swiss chard, spinach, or mustard greens, the technique is similar, making it easy to sauté these nutritious veggies on a regular basis. This dish was inspired by the Greek phyllo treat, *spanakopita*. The grated nutmeg and feta provide subtle hints of the classic Mediterranean dish. I particularly love this served alongside Chicken Piccata (page 144).

SERVES 4 • PREP 10 minutes • COOK 10 minutes

1 In a large skillet set over medium-high heat, melt the butter, then add the oil. Add the shallot and cook, stirring, until softened and fragrant, 2 minutes. Add the garlic and cook until the garlic is golden brown, 1 to 2 minutes. Add the nutmeg, 1/2 teaspoon salt, and 1/4 teaspoon pepper. Stir in the spinach and cook, stirring frequently, until the spinach turns bright green and wilts slightly, 1 to 2 minutes. Season to taste with salt and pepper.

2 Transfer the spinach to a serving dish and top with the cheese. Serve immediately.

seasonal ingredients

I like to let seasonal ingredients drive my direction in the kitchen. They're fresh, full of flavor, and usually less expensive than out-of-season fruits and vegetables. Plus they're a great way to break up a dinner routine that is starting to feel a little tired. For example, after the long winter months full of braising and comfort foods and root vegetables, the arrival of spring vegetables at the market is a signal that it's time to switch up my cooking a bit, using quicker techniques and lighter recipes for these more delicate foods. I like to keep a list of what's in season hanging in my kitchen as a friendly reminder of what to look for at the market, making sure to catch those ingredients that have a smaller seasonal window. Enjoying these fruits and vegetables at their peak makes the most of their freshness, flavor, and nutritional value. Participating in Community Supported Agriculture (CSA), where you can purchase local, seasonal food directly from a farmer, or shopping at your local farmers' market is an easy way to stay on top of what is at its peak.

SAUTÉED BRUSSELS SPROUTS

WITH MAPLE AND PECANS

SERVES **4** • PREP **10 minutes** • COOK **10 minutes**

1½ pounds Brussels sprouts, trimmed

2 tablespoons extra-virgin olive oil

1 small shallot, finely chopped

1 garlic clove, minced

2 tablespoons pure maple syrup

½ cup pecans, toasted (see page 203) and roughly chopped

Kosher salt and cracked black pepper

Brussels sprouts are terribly misunderstood. They are one of my favorite vegetables and I always look forward to their season in winter. My love affair with Brussels sprouts began a few years ago when I started to roast them simply with just olive oil, salt, and pepper. After preparing them this classic way for years, I thought that it was time to switch things up. So I began slicing them into fine ribbons and sautéing them to make one of the quickest side dishes ever. Adding the maple syrup is the real secret to this recipe: It slightly caramelizes the Brussels sprouts and lends just a hint of sweetness. The pecans pair really nicely with the maple flavor, and their crunch adds great texture to the dish. It's good enough to turn any Brussels sprouts hater into a true believer.

1 Halve the Brussels sprouts lengthwise and thinly slice them crosswise into fine ribbons. You should have about 6 cups.

2 In a large skillet set over medium-high heat, heat the oil. Add the shallot and cook for 1 minute. Add the garlic and cook for 30 seconds. Add the Brussels sprouts and cook, stirring, until tender, about 5 minutes. Add the maple syrup and pecans and cook for 1 minute. Season to taste with salt and pepper and serve hot.

SAUTÉED BRUSSELS SPROUTS WITH LEMON AND CAPERS For a more savory version, replace the maple syrup and pecans with 1 tablespoon capers, ¼ cup grated Parmesan cheese, and the juice of ½ lemon.

SWEET CORNBREAD

SERVES **8** · PREP **10 minutes** · COOK **40 minutes**

½ cup (1 stick) unsalted butter, melted

⅔ cup sugar

2 large eggs

1 cup buttermilk

½ teaspoon baking soda

1 cup cornmeal

1 cup all-purpose flour

½ teaspoon kosher salt

People can be particular about how they like their cornbread. This old-fashioned recipe is a great base, easily adaptable to one's own preferences. In my opinion this version is plenty sweet and rich and delightfully cakey, but you could add more sugar, another egg, or more butter if you want to make it even more indulgent. Add crisped bacon, chopped chiles, fresh herbs, spices like cumin or cayenne, grated cheese, or even fresh or canned corn, if you like. Fresh out of the oven and slathered with butter and honey, this simple cornbread is hard to beat.

1 Preheat the oven to 375°F. Butter an 8-inch square baking dish.

2 In a large bowl, combine the melted butter and sugar. Whisk in the eggs, one at a time, and beat well.

3 In a small bowl or measuring cup, combine the buttermilk and baking soda. Stir the buttermilk mixture into the sugar mixture. Stir in the cornmeal, flour, and salt until only a few lumps remain. Pour the batter into the prepared pan.

4 Bake until a cake tester inserted into the center of the cornbread comes out clean, 30 to 35 minutes. Let cool slightly before serving.

TOASTED VERMICELLI PILAF

SERVES **4** • PREP **10 minutes** • COOK **35 minutes**

2½ cups low-sodium chicken broth

⅓ cup (⅔ stick) unsalted butter

1 teaspoon kosher salt

¼ teaspoon cracked black pepper

2 tablespoons extra-virgin olive oil

½ cup broken vermicelli (2 ounces)

1 cup long-grain white rice

1 tablespoon chopped fresh flat-leaf parsley

Admittedly, this recipe was created to mimic one of my favorite prepared side dishes that comes from a box, sometimes known as "the San Francisco treat." I prefer my homemade version, which includes both rice and vermicelli that have been broken, toasted, and then cooked in chicken broth. The contrasting textures are great together and the dish goes well with just about any main course. If you don't have vermicelli on hand, consider using any thin pasta like angel hair.

1   In a medium saucepan set over medium-high heat, combine the chicken broth, butter, salt, and pepper. Bring the mixture to a simmer, cover, and keep at a low simmer over medium-low heat.

2   Meanwhile, in a heavy skillet set over medium low heat, heat the oil. Add the vermicelli and cook, stirring constantly, until the pasta is golden brown all over, about 5 minutes. Add the rice and cook, stirring, until the rice grains change from pale white to bright white, about 7 minutes.

3   Carefully pour the simmering broth mixture over the rice and vermicelli. Scrape down the sides of the pan, making sure that all of the rice is submerged in broth. Bring the mixture to a low simmer, cover, and cook for 15 minutes. Uncover and cook until all of the liquid is absorbed, about 5 minutes longer.

4   Add the parsley and fluff the vermicelli and rice with a fork. Season to taste with salt and pepper. Transfer to a serving dish and serve hot.

ESSENTIAL
QUINOA PILAF

WITH VARIATIONS

2 tablespoons
extra-virgin olive oil,
butter, or vegetable oil

½ onion or 1 shallot,
finely chopped

1 cup quinoa, rinsed and
drained thoroughly

2 cups broth or water

1½ tablespoons chopped
fresh parsley (or other
herbs, spices, or
seasonings, to taste)

Kosher salt and cracked
black pepper

Quinoa has a lot going for it: It's fast cooking, packed with protein, and has a wonderfully nutty flavor that pairs really well with a variety of ingredients. It can be steamed or, in this case, treated like rice to make a pilaf. Once you become familiar with this simple technique for cooking quinoa, you can start to tweak it by adding a variety of both fresh ingredients and pantry staples to make it a little bit different each time (see variations).

SERVES **4** • PREP **10 minutes** • COOK **25 minutes**

1 In a heavy saucepan set over medium-high heat, heat the oil. Add the onion and cook, stirring, until translucent and fragrant, about 2 minutes. Add the quinoa and stir well. Add the broth and bring to a simmer. Cover the pan and cook until the liquid is absorbed and the quinoa is tender, about 20 minutes.

2 Stir in the parsley, season to taste with salt and pepper, transfer to a serving dish, and serve.

COCONUT-LIME QUINOA Sauté the onion in vegetable oil. Add the quinoa and instead of 2 cups broth, use a combination of 1 cup coconut milk and 1 cup chicken broth. Cook as directed. Omit the parsley and season the cooked quinoa with 1½ tablespoons fresh lime juice and ¼ teaspoon grated lime zest.

LEMON-THYME QUINOA Sauté a shallot in butter. Add the quinoa, and instead of 2 cups broth, use a combination of ¼ cup fresh lemon juice and 1¾ cups chicken broth. Cook as directed. Season the cooked quinoa with 1 teaspoon chopped fresh thyme leaves instead of the parsley.

MEDITERRANEAN QUINOA Cook the quinoa as directed. Add ½ cup chopped tomatoes, ¼ cup chopped Kalamata olives, 2 tablespoons fresh lemon juice, and ¼ teaspoon grated lemon zest and mix gently. Top with ⅓ cup crumbled feta cheese.

BACON AND BLUE CHEESE TWICE-BAKED POTATOES

SERVES **12** • PREP **20 minutes** • COOK **1 hour 15 minutes**

6 russet (baking) potatoes

Extra-virgin olive oil

¼ pound thick-cut bacon (about 4 slices)

1 cup (4 ounces) crumbled blue cheese

¾ cup sour cream

⅔ cup half-and-half, plus more as needed

¼ cup (½ stick) unsalted butter, at room temperature

1 bunch scallions, chopped

Kosher salt and cracked black pepper

My grandma Karen has been serving these twice-baked potatoes for as long as I can remember. Each bite captures the creamy and rich interior and crispy-skinned exterior that make the potato so beloved. The sky is the limit when it comes to additions. I love bacon, perhaps typically, and blue cheese, but have also been known to add sautéed onions to these as well (see variations).

1 Preheat the oven to 400°F.

2 Scrub the potatoes and dry them thoroughly. Drizzle the potatoes with oil, coating them evenly, and put them on a baking sheet. Bake until the skins are crisp and the potatoes are fork-tender, about 1 hour. Transfer the potatoes to a wire rack and let cool just until you can handle them. Leave the oven on.

3 Meanwhile, in a skillet set over medium heat, cook the bacon until the fat has rendered and the bacon is crisp, 8 to 10 minutes. Transfer the crisped bacon to a paper towel–lined plate. When cool enough to handle, crumble the bacon. Set aside.

4 Halve the potatoes lengthwise. Holding a potato half in your hand, scoop out the flesh into a large bowl with the tip of a spoon, leaving about ¼ inch of flesh lining each potato skin. Return the potato skins to the baking sheet. Bake until crisp, about 8 minutes. Remove from the oven and turn the oven to broil.

5 Meanwhile, using a fork, mash the potato flesh. Add the crumbled bacon, ½ cup of the blue cheese, the sour cream, half-and-half, and butter. If the mixture seems too thick, add more half-and-half, 1 tablespoon at a time. Stir in the scallions (reserving a few for garnish) and season to taste with salt and pepper.

6 Working carefully with the hot potatoes, fill each shell with the filling and top with the remaining ½ cup blue cheese. Broil until the cheese has started to melt, 3 to 5 minutes.

7 Garnish with the reserved scallions and serve.

TWICE-BAKED SWEET POTATOES Substitute sweet potatoes or yams for the russet potatoes and decrease the initial baking time by 15 minutes.

TWICE-BAKED SWEET POTATOES WITH BROWN SUGAR AND PECANS For an even sweeter version, mix the scooped sweet potato or yam flesh with 2 tablespoons light brown sugar, 1 tablespoon butter, and ¼ cup pecans instead of the bacon, scallions, and cheese. Fill and broil as directed.

SCALLOPED SWEET POTATOES

SERVES **6** • PREP **15 minutes** • COOK **40 minutes**

2 tablespoons unsalted butter

1 large yellow onion, finely chopped

2 garlic cloves, minced

1¼ cups heavy cream

¼ cup low-sodium chicken broth

2 teaspoons chopped fresh thyme leaves

1½ teaspoons kosher salt

½ teaspoon cracked black pepper

2 pounds sweet potatoes, peeled and cut into ⅛-inch-thick slices

2 ounces Gruyère cheese, shredded (½ cup)

For an easy twist on the classic potato gratin, I turn to sweet potatoes, which I simmer in cream and broth, top with a little cheese, and bake until bubbling. The earthiness of the sweet potato is the perfect balance for the richness and the nuttiness of the Gruyère cheese. This simple method is a great one to follow when making gratins with different potato varieties, like buttery Yukon Golds.

1 Preheat the oven to 375°F.

2 In a cast-iron skillet set over medium-high heat, melt the butter. Add the onion and cook, stirring, until softened and beginning to brown, about 5 minutes. Add the garlic and cook for 1 minute. Stir in the cream, broth, and thyme, and season with the salt and pepper. Add half of the sweet potato slices in a flat layer, then half of the cheese, then the remaining sweet potatoes. Bring to a simmer; do not stir. Reduce the heat to medium-low and cook for 5 minutes longer. Top with the remaining cheese and transfer the skillet to the oven.

3 Bake until bubbling and the surface begins to brown, about 15 minutes. Let cool for 10 minutes before serving.

CHEESY
SMASHED POTATOES

1½ pounds small Yukon
Gold potatoes

Kosher salt

3 tablespoons unsalted
butter

½ cup half-and-half

4 ounces cream cheese,
at room temperature

Cracked black pepper

I love mashed potatoes but I don't have the space in my kitchen for a potato ricer, a tool necessary to ensure smooth and pillowy results every time. My solution is to make smashed potatoes, which are every bit as good when it comes to flavor, but don't require removing the skins or using a special or hard-to-clean kitchen tool. I've used everything from a classic potato masher to a slotted spoon or large fork to coarsely mash these potatoes. They also have cream cheese to thank for their deliciousness—it makes them super creamy and full of flavor.

1 Put the potatoes in a large pot, cover with cold water, and salt generously. Cover and bring to a boil over high heat. Cook until the potatoes are fork-tender, 20 to 30 minutes. Drain the potatoes, return them to the pot, and let them dry in the still-hot pan, about 2 minutes.

2 Meanwhile, in a small saucepan set over low heat, melt the butter. Stir in the half-and-half.

3 Add the butter-cream mixture and cream cheese to the potatoes. Season to taste with salt and pepper. Smash the potatoes with a potato masher or large fork. Taste and add more salt and pepper, if needed. Serve warm.

CREAMY CAULIFLOWER PUREE

Vegetable purees are a wonderful, healthier alternative to mashed potatoes, shaking up your dinner plate a bit while filling the same satisfying role. They still use those rich ingredients that we all love—like butter, cream, and cheese—but they can be made with significantly less. Cooking the cauliflower in chicken broth gives the dish a delicious flavor base. Finally, this recipe is faster than making classic mashed potatoes, and you don't even have to worry about lumps!

SERVES 4 • **PREP 10 minutes** • **COOK 10 minutes**

1 (2-pound) head cauliflower, cut into florets

4 cups low-sodium chicken broth

2 tablespoons heavy cream

2 tablespoons unsalted butter, at room temperature

2 ounces sharp cheddar cheese, shredded (½ cup)

Kosher salt and cracked black pepper

1 tablespoon finely chopped fresh chives, for garnish

1 In a medium saucepan set over medium-high heat, combine the cauliflower and chicken broth. Bring to a simmer and cook until the florets are tender, 8 to 10 minutes.

2 Drain the cauliflower, reserving ½ cup of the cooking liquid. Transfer the cauliflower to a blender or food processor and blend until smooth, adding cooking liquid as needed to achieve a smooth consistency. Add the cream, butter, and cheese and continue blending until combined. Season to taste with salt and pepper.

3 Garnish with the chives and serve hot.

ROOT VEGETABLE PUREE Once you get in the habit of making this painfully easy side dish, you'll be pureeing everything, subbing in celery root, parsnips, or rutabagas for the cauliflower.

SAUSAGE, APPLE, AND PEAR DRESSING
WITH CRANBERRIES

SERVES 12 • PREP 20 minutes • COOK 50 minutes

1 pound sweet Italian sausage, casings removed

3 small leeks (white and light green parts only), thinly sliced (about 1½ cups)

4 ribs celery, finely chopped (about 2 cups)

1 Granny Smith apple, cored and cut into ¼-inch cubes

1 Bosc pear, cored and cut into ¼-inch cubes

1 tablespoon chopped fresh thyme

1 tablespoon chopped fresh sage

1 tablespoon chopped fresh flat-leaf parsley, plus more for garnish

1 teaspoon kosher salt

1 teaspoon cracked black pepper

2 cups low-sodium chicken broth

1 (12-ounce) bag seasoned bread stuffing cubes

1 cup dried cranberries

4 large eggs, beaten

Everyone tends to think about stuffing only when it comes to the holidays, but why not consider making it as a side dish throughout the fall and winter months? I love making it to pair with a roast chicken or turkey breast for a weeknight meal. It reheats well, making it a great option to enjoy throughout the week. The apples, pears, and cranberries are so delicious and sweet; the variety of fresh herbs and fennel sausage keeps it savory; and the texture is out of this world, with a browned, crispy top and soft, rich center.

1 Preheat the oven to 350°F. Butter a 9 × 13-inch baking dish.

2 In a large skillet set over medium-high heat, cook the sausage, breaking it up with a wooden spoon, until browned through, about 5 minutes. Add the leeks, celery, apple, and pear and cook, stirring, until fragrant and softened, about 5 minutes. Stir in the thyme, sage, parsley, salt, and pepper and cook for 1 minute. Add the chicken broth and scrape up any bits from the bottom of the pan, cooking for 1 minute longer. Remove the pan from the heat and cool slightly.

3 In a large bowl, combine the stuffing cubes and cooled sausage mixture. Add the cranberries and eggs and mix well. Transfer the mixture to the prepared baking dish.

4 Bake until golden brown on top, 30 to 35 minutes. Let cool before serving garnished with parsley.

LEMON RISOTTO

WITH PEAS AND PARMESAN

SERVES 4 • PREP 15 minutes • COOK 40 minutes

4½ cups low-sodium chicken broth

3 tablespoons unsalted butter

2 large shallots, finely chopped (about ½ cup)

1 cup Arborio rice

¾ cup dry white wine

1 cup frozen petite peas, thawed

Grated zest and juice of ½ lemon

¾ cup grated Parmesan cheese

½ cup shredded low-moisture mozzarella cheese

Kosher salt and cracked black pepper

Making a proper risotto takes time, attention, and a lot of love, but the end result is so worth it. It's important to have all of your ingredients prepared and ready to go before you start. Then it's all about the stirring, which rubs the starch off the Arborio rice, creating a great creamy texture and sauciness—a wooden spoon will get into the curved parts of the pan while the handle stays cool. I love the bright lemony flavor in this dish and the fact that I can use petite peas from the stash that I always have in my freezer.

1 In a medium saucepan set over medium-high heat, bring the chicken broth to a simmer.

2 In a separate heavy saucepan set over medium-high heat, melt the butter. Add the shallots and cook until fragrant and translucent, about 2 minutes. Add the rice and lightly toast, stirring to coat it in the butter and shallots, about 1 minute. Add the wine and cook, stirring until it has been absorbed, about 3 minutes.

3 Reduce the heat to medium. Using a ladle, add enough of the warm chicken broth to just cover the rice. Cook, stirring constantly, until the broth is completely absorbed, about 5 minutes. Repeat the process 3 more times. Once all of the chicken broth has been added and the rice is tender, add the peas, lemon zest, and lemon juice and stir well.

4 Remove the pan from the heat and stir in the Parmesan and mozzarella. Season to taste with salt and pepper. Serve immediately.

CREAMED CORN

3 tablespoons unsalted butter

6 ears corn, shucked, kernels cut and "milk" scraped from the cob (about 6 cups)

Kosher salt and cracked black pepper

2 cups heavy cream

1 tablespoon sugar

Fresh corn is hands down my favorite vegetable. I love its sweet, juicy flavor and the ease of adding it to recipes or just enjoying it on its own. Creamed corn, which calls for fresh corn kernels and corn "milk," showcases the most intense corn flavor possible, in my opinion. To remove the kernels from the cob, stand each cob up in a shallow baking dish and saw down the length of the cob with the tip of a chef's knife, using a back-and-forth motion; this way, as they are cut, the kernels land conveniently in the dish. The "milk" is the juice and pulp that you scrape from the stripped cobs with the back of the knife. I think this very important ingredient adds more creaminess and perfect thickened texture to the final dish than the cream itself!

1 In a large skillet set over medium heat, melt the butter. Add the corn kernels and corn "milk" to the pan. Season liberally with salt and pepper and cook, stirring, for 5 minutes. Add the cream and sugar, bring the mixture to a simmer, and cook until the liquid has reduced by half, 5 to 7 minutes. Remove the pan from the heat.

2 Carefully transfer half of the mixture to a food processor or blender and puree until smooth. (Alternatively, use an immersion blender and blend to the desired consistency.) Return the puree to the pan and put the pan over low heat. Taste and add more salt and pepper, if needed. Serve hot.

ROASTED ROOT VEGETABLES
WITH CIDER VINAIGRETTE

VEGETABLES

¼ cup extra-virgin olive oil

1 large sweet potato, peeled, halved lengthwise, and cut crosswise into 1-inch pieces

2 large carrots, sliced into ½-inch-thick rounds

2 large parsnips, peeled and sliced into ½-inch-thick rounds

1 medium red onion, cut into 1-inch-thick wedges

5 garlic cloves, smashed

1 tablespoon fresh thyme leaves, chopped

Kosher salt and cracked black pepper

CIDER VINAIGRETTE

2 tablespoons extra-virgin olive oil

2 tablespoons apple cider vinegar

1 teaspoon Dijon mustard

1 teaspoon honey

1 small shallot, finely chopped

Kosher salt and cracked black pepper

SERVES **4** • PREP **20 minutes** • COOK **45 minutes**

If you've never roasted root vegetables before, you're in for a treat. Roasting brings out the natural sweetness and intensifies the flavors of these hardy cellar stalwarts. The bright and acidic cider vinaigrette is a great pairing for the rich, caramelized earthiness of the veggies. One note: Be sure to cut harder vegetables like parsnips and carrots a bit smaller than softer ones like onions, so that everything cooks through in the same amount of time.

1 **For the vegetables:** Preheat the oven to 425°F. Put the oven rack in the top third of the oven. Line a baking sheet with foil or grease with olive oil.

2 In a large bowl, combine the oil, sweet potato, carrots, parsnips, onion, garlic, and thyme. Season liberally with salt and pepper and toss to coat. Transfer to the prepared baking sheet.

3 Roast, turning once halfway through, until the vegetables are tender and starting to brown, about 45 minutes.

4 **For the vinaigrette:** Meanwhile, in a small bowl, whisk together the oil, vinegar, mustard, honey, and shallot. Season to taste with salt and pepper.

5 Transfer the roasted vegetables to a serving bowl and toss with the vinaigrette. Serve warm.

HARICOTS VERTS AMANDINE

1½ pounds haricots verts
(French string beans),
stem ends removed

3 tablespoons unsalted
butter

1½ tablespoons
extra-virgin olive oil

2 shallots, finely chopped

Kosher salt and cracked
black pepper

Grated zest and juice of
½ lemon

¼ cup whole almonds,
toasted (see page 203)
and finely chopped

This recipe is a classic and should be in every cook's repertoire:
It was one of the first side dishes I learned how to make. The
delicacy of the haricots verts (you could substitute green beans,
though you'll have a slightly heartier dish) balances perfectly
with the acidity of the lemon and richness of the butter and
almonds. The French technique of blanching and shocking the
vegetables (see page 84) is one that you will use over and over in
the kitchen. The secret to getting the crunchy nutty almond flavor
in every single bite is to toast and finely chop the almonds and
then toss thoroughly with the haricots verts.

1 Bring a large pot of salted water to a boil. Add the
   haricots verts and blanch until crisp but tender, 2 to
   3 minutes. Immediately drain the beans and run cold
   water over them, or plunge them into an ice bath to cool
   and stop the cooking process. Drain and dry completely.

2 In a large skillet set over medium heat, melt the butter,
   then add the oil. Add the shallots, season with salt and
   pepper, and cook, stirring occasionally, until the shallots
   begin to brown, 3 to 5 minutes. Add the beans, lemon
   zest, and lemon juice. Cook to heat the beans through,
   1 to 2 minutes.

3 Remove the pan from the heat and season to taste with
   salt and pepper. Toss with the almonds and transfer to a
   serving dish. Serve warm.

DESSERTS & SWEETS

CHOCOLATE CHIP COOKIES

MAKES **2 dozen** • PREP **10 minutes** • COOK **15 minutes**

1 cup (2 sticks)
unsalted butter, at room
temperature

1 cup packed light brown
sugar

⅓ cup granulated sugar

2 large eggs

2 teaspoons vanilla
extract

2½ cups all-purpose flour

1 teaspoon baking
powder

1 teaspoon baking soda

¾ teaspoon kosher salt

1 (12-ounce) package
milk chocolate chips
(2 cups)

I spent years trying to create the perfect chocolate chip cookie. One day, when I was cooking a big batch of recipes in the Food Network kitchens, I tested a hunch—extra brown sugar and egg—and I've never looked back. I can't rave enough about the texture of these cookies: slightly crispy on the edges, soft in the center, and just the right proportion of chocolate chips. I especially love the way the vanilla really comes through. Someday, when my kids are involved in bake sales at school, these are the cookies I will make. But since all of the ingredients can easily be found in my pantry any time of the year, which is equally dangerous and wonderful, I don't need to wait for a bake sale to make them.

1 Preheat the oven to 350°F. Line 2 baking sheets with parchment paper.

2 Using an electric mixer, cream together the butter and both sugars, mixing until pale yellow and fluffy, about 3 minutes. Mix in the eggs, one at a time, then beat in the vanilla.

3 In a separate bowl, whisk together the flour, baking powder, baking soda, and salt. Slowly beat the flour mixture into the butter mixture. Stir in the chocolate chips. Roll the dough into balls about 2 tablespoons each and place them 2 inches apart on the prepared baking sheets.

4 Bake until the edges just start to brown, 12 to 14 minutes. Transfer the cookies to a wire rack to cool. (Cooled cookies will keep in an airtight container at room temperature for up to 3 days.)

GINGERBREAD COOKIES

MAKES **15** · PREP **10 minutes plus chilling time** · COOK **15 minutes**

⅓ cup (⅔ stick) **unsalted butter, at room temperature**

1 cup packed light brown sugar

1½ cups molasses

7 cups all-purpose flour

2 teaspoons baking soda

1 teaspoon kosher salt

2 teaspoons ground ginger

1 teaspoon ground allspice

1 teaspoon ground cinnamon

1 teaspoon ground cloves

The holidays aren't complete until my aunt Kim shows up with multiple platters of these gingerbread cookies. We go through dozens every year and, admittedly, I probably eat a half dozen single-handedly within the first day or two. The secret is in the balanced combination of spices; every bite has a robust, full, spicy flavor. The cookies have outstanding chewy, soft texture, which comes from rolling the dough thick.

1 In the bowl of a stand mixer fitted with the paddle attachment, cream together the butter and sugar on medium speed until it begins to lighten in color, about 3 minutes. Add the molasses and ⅔ cup cold water and mix well.

2 In a separate bowl, whisk together the flour, baking soda, salt, ginger, allspice, cinnamon, and cloves. With the mixer running on medium speed, slowly add the flour mixture until the dough comes together. Turn the dough out onto a piece of plastic wrap, form it into a disc, and wrap tightly. Chill the dough for at least 30 minutes before rolling; it must be cold.

3 Preheat the oven to 350°F. Line 2 baking sheets with parchment paper.

4 On a well-floured surface, roll out the chilled dough to a ½-inch thickness. Cut out shapes with a gingerbread man cookie cutter and transfer them to the prepared pans, spacing them 2 inches apart. Reroll the scraps to cut out more cookies if desired.

5 Bake one tray at a time on the center rack in the oven until the edges start to crisp, 10 to 12 minutes. Transfer the cookies to a wire rack to cool.

SIMPLE SUGAR COOKIES

1¼ cups all-purpose flour

½ teaspoon baking powder

½ teaspoon kosher salt

½ cup (1 stick) unsalted butter, at room temperature

1 cup granulated sugar

¼ cup packed light brown sugar

1 large egg

1 teaspoon vanilla extract

Despite being made from the simplest ingredients, these tender sugar cookies right out of the oven are enough to make me swoon. Rolling the portioned dough in additional sugar just before baking contributes to a sweet and crisp exterior. You can skip this step to create a smooth-surfaced cookie perfect for icing or frosting (see page 219). If you're looking for a cutout sugar cookie, chill the dough, roll thin, and cut it into desired shapes before baking (double the recipe if you want to have enough dough to make about 2 dozen cookies, depending on the size of your cutters). This recipe is one that I make all the time and use as a base for variations to fill out my cookie platter.

MAKES **2 dozen** • PREP **10 minutes** • COOK **15 minutes**

1 Preheat the oven to 350°F. Line 2 baking sheets with parchment paper.

2 In a medium bowl, whisk together the flour, baking powder, and salt.

3 In a large bowl, using an electric mixer, beat together the butter, ½ cup of the granulated sugar, and the brown sugar, mixing until pale yellow and fluffy, about 3 minutes. Beat in the egg and vanilla. Slowly incorporate the flour mixture into the butter-sugar mixture and mix well.

4 Put the remaining ½ cup granulated sugar in a small bowl. Using slightly wet hands, roll the dough into heaping tablespoon-size balls, roll them in the sugar, and put them on the baking sheets, spacing them 2 inches apart.

5 Baking one sheet at a time, bake just until the edges start to brown, 10 to 12 minutes. Transfer the cookies to a wire rack to cool. (Cooled cookies will keep in an airtight container for up to 3 days.)

LEMON
BARS

My husband is convinced that I have a heavy hand when it comes to working with lemon in the kitchen. I'm guilty as charged. I love the bright acidic flavor of citrus, especially during the colder months when food can get so heavy. While lemon bars are delicious any time of the year, I particularly love making them in the winter when citrus is abundant. When it comes to the intricacies of lemon bars, I'm equally opinionated: I fall into the camp of equal lemon curd and crust layers; I prefer biting into a lemon bar that is just as much buttery crust as it is luscious lemon filling. One of the secrets for making the lemon filling is really whipping some air into the eggs when you beat them. It takes an extra minute or two, but the light and fluffy result is worth it.

MAKES 16 • **PREP 20 minutes** • **COOK 50 minutes**

SHORTBREAD CRUST

1 cup all-purpose flour

⅓ cup powdered sugar

1½ tablespoons cornstarch

1 tablespoon grated lemon zest

½ teaspoon kosher salt

½ cup (1 stick) unsalted butter, chilled and cut into cubes

LEMON FILLING

1½ cups powdered sugar, plus more for topping

⅓ cup all-purpose flour

½ teaspoon baking powder

3 large eggs, at room temperature

1 tablespoon grated lemon zest

½ cup fresh lemon juice (from 4 lemons)

1 **For the shortbread crust:** Preheat the oven to 350°F. Butter an 8-inch square baking pan and line it with parchment paper.

2 In a medium bowl, whisk together the flour, powdered sugar, cornstarch, lemon zest, and salt. Cut in the butter using two forks, a pastry blender, or your hands, or by pulsing in a food processor, until the mixture is crumbly. Gently bring the dough together with your hands, kneading it slightly. Put the dough into the prepared baking dish and press it into the bottom.

3 Bake just until starting to brown, about 20 minutes. Remove the pan from the oven and let cool slightly on a wire rack while you make the filling. (Keep in mind that the crust should still be warm when the filling goes on top.) Leave the oven on.

4 **For the lemon filling:** Meanwhile, in a medium bowl, whisk together the powdered sugar, flour, and baking powder.

5 Using an electric mixer, beat the eggs on high speed until their volume has tripled in size, 2 to 3 minutes. With the mixer running on medium speed, add the powdered sugar mixture to the eggs and mix just until blended. Add the lemon zest and juice, mixing just until incorporated.

6 Pour the filling over the crust and bake until the filling is set in the center, 25 to 30 minutes. Cool completely on a wire rack.

7 Sift a little powdered sugar over the top, and slice into bars. (The bars will keep in an airtight container for up to 2 days.)

MEYER LEMON BARS If I'm really treating myself, I'll make this exact same recipe using Meyer lemons instead of standard lemons, which will give the bars a slightly sweeter, more aromatic flavor. Meyer lemons are a bit more expensive and harder to track down, but their sweeter taste with distinct floral notes can't be beat. You can also try this recipe with other citrus such as lime, orange, or grapefruit.

zester

My zester gets a lot of use in my kitchen. As opposed to a regular stand-up cheese grater, a Microplane (my favorite brand) is easy to use, store, and clean. The fine grates produce a pillow of fluffy, even, snowflake-like zest or cheese with just a few swipes. Beyond citrus zest and hard cheeses, I use my zester for more unsuspecting things like spices (nutmeg especially), ginger, and garlic. If you hate mincing garlic, grating it is a fantastic alternative: You can be done in just a second (grate it right into the pan or pot, if you like) and you won't need to wash a knife or a cutting board. My zester even makes its way to the dinner table with me to top off our dinner with a light dusting of cheese. Whether I'm making dinner or baking, I reach for this tool on a regular basis and can't imagine functioning as efficiently in my kitchen without it.

HONEY CORN

As you may or may not know, Utah is the beehive state, which may account for my special love of honey. Honey corn is a signature treat where I come from, served everywhere from the state fair to small, cozy craft shops along the Wasatch Front. Just as the season begins to transition from late summer to early fall, I find myself whipping up a batch of this hometown favorite. This soft, sweet popcorn is ooey, gooey, and wonderful served warm, just after you finish making it. It's also delicious served over ice cream or molded into popcorn balls; keep it in mind when looking for a gift to give from your kitchen, especially around the holidays. A candy thermometer is recommended for this recipe. It acts as an insurance policy when making perfect caramel, and therefore perfect, caramel-y honey corn.

MAKES **25 cups** · PREP **10 minutes** · COOK **10 minutes**

24 cups popped corn (from about 1 cup popcorn kernels)

1½ cups roasted salted peanuts

4 cups sugar

1 cup (2 sticks) unsalted butter

1 cup heavy cream

1 cup honey

1 teaspoon baking soda

1 Line 2 baking sheets with foil, wrapping the foil over the outside edges of the baking sheet.

2 Divide the popcorn and peanuts evenly between the 2 sheets.

3 In a large soup pot or Dutch oven set over medium-high heat, combine the sugar, butter, cream, and honey. Bring to a boil, then reduce the heat to medium. Clip a candy thermometer on the side of the pot. Gently boil the mixture until it reaches the soft-ball stage, about 234°F. Remove the pot from the heat and, while stirring constantly, add the baking soda.

4 Pour the sugar mixture evenly over the 2 baking sheets of popcorn and mix well with large spoons (the sugar mixture will be very hot). Let cool slightly and enjoy warm or at room temperature. (Store in an airtight container for up to 2 days.)

FUDGE MINT BROWNIES

BROWNIES

MAKES **24** • PREP **30 minutes plus freezing time** • COOK **40 minutes**

Cooking spray

1 cup (2 sticks) unsalted butter, melted

3 cups sugar

1 tablespoon vanilla extract

4 large eggs

1½ cups all-purpose flour

1 cup unsweetened cocoa powder

1 teaspoon kosher salt

1 cup walnuts (optional), toasted (see page 203) and chopped

CHOCOLATE ICING

¼ cup (½ stick) unsalted butter, at room temperature

3 tablespoons whole milk, plus more as needed

2 cups powdered sugar

¼ cup unsweetened cocoa powder

¼ teaspoon kosher salt

I loved my college days at Brigham Young University. It didn't take long after my first semester for me to discover the infamous BYU Creamery, known for having the best ice cream around and for their famous mint brownies, to which quite a few freshman can likely attribute their "freshman 15." To pay homage to the best of BYU baking, I created my own version of these decadent brownies, which put the fudge in fudgy with their soft center and crispy edges. The thin layer of mint icing followed by another thin layer of chocolate icing together create a creamy top with just enough mintiness to finish off these brownies perfectly. (See page 219 for more tips on frosting.)

1 **For the brownies:** Preheat the oven to 350°F. Coat a 9 × 13-inch baking pan with cooking spray. Line the dish with foil so there is a 1-inch overhang on all sides. Coat the foil with cooking spray.

2 In a large bowl, combine the melted butter, sugar, and vanilla. Using an electric mixer, beat in the eggs, one at a time, mixing well after each addition.

3 In a separate bowl, sift together the flour, cocoa powder, and salt. Gradually stir the flour mixture into the egg-butter mixture until blended. Stir in the walnuts (if using). Spread the batter evenly into the prepared baking dish.

4 Bake until a cake tester inserted comes out clean, 30 to 35 minutes. Transfer the pan to a wire rack and let cool completely.

MINT ICING

¼ cup (½ stick)
unsalted butter, at room
temperature

3 tablespoons whole
milk, plus more as
needed

2 teaspoons light corn
syrup

½ teaspoon mint extract

1 to 2 drops green food
coloring (optional)

2 cups powdered sugar

¼ teaspoon kosher salt

5 **For the chocolate icing:** In a bowl, combine the butter, milk, powdered sugar, cocoa powder, and salt. Using an electric mixer, beat until smooth, adding more milk if the icing is too thick.

6 **For the mint icing:** In a bowl, combine the butter, milk, corn syrup, mint extract, food coloring (if using), powdered sugar, and salt. Using an electric mixer, beat until smooth, adding more milk if the icing is too thick.

7 Frost the pan of cooled brownies with the mint icing, cover with plastic wrap, and put in the freezer for 30 minutes to set the icing. Remove the pan from the freezer and top the mint icing with a layer of the chocolate icing. Freeze the brownies for 10 to 15 minutes.

8 Cut into bars and serve. (The brownies will keep in an airtight container in the refrigerator for up to 3 days.)

toasting nuts

Toasting nuts is a simple way to boost their flavor and add some extra crunch. A toasted nut has a deeper nutty and earthy flavor. For big batches, preheat the oven to 400°F and spread the nuts evenly in a single layer on a baking sheet. Bake, carefully shaking the pan halfway through cooking, until the color has deepened and you can smell them, about 10 minutes. Be sure to immediately transfer them to a plate to cool so they don't continue cooking on the hot pan. Alternatively, you can toast smaller batches of nuts in a dry skillet over medium heat— keep a close eye on them and shake the pan constantly to prevent any burning. Only toast as many nuts as you need for a given recipe, as the toasted flavor will diminish with time.

BANANA SPLIT
ICEBOX CAKE

SERVES **8** • PREP **20 minutes plus chilling time**

¾ pound strawberries, hulled and sliced

6 bananas, sliced

2½ cups chilled heavy cream

1 cup powdered sugar

½ teaspoon vanilla extract

2 (9-ounce) packages chocolate wafer cookies

¼ cup chocolate syrup or sauce

3 tablespoons chopped toasted peanuts (see page 203)

1 maraschino cherry, for garnish (optional)

One of the best things about making an icebox cake is that no baking is involved. The process of layering cookies and whipped cream or custard, followed by chilling for a few hours in the "icebox"—i.e., the refrigerator—creates a dessert with a moist cake texture. This retro dessert comes together quickly, yet still manages a major wow factor both visually and tastewise.

1   In a blender, puree ½ cup of the strawberries with 1 tablespoon water until thick and smooth. Set aside another ½ cup sliced strawberries and ½ cup sliced banana for garnish.

2   Using an electric mixer, whip the cream until soft peaks form, 3 to 5 minutes. Add the sugar, vanilla, and strawberry puree and continue whipping until slightly stiff peaks form, about 2 minutes more.

3   In a 9-inch springform pan, arrange a layer of cookies (about 16) in a circle, overlapping them to fit. Spread about one-fifth of the strawberry whipped cream over the cookies, making sure to cover them completely. Top with about one-quarter each of the strawberry and banana slices. Repeat the layering to make a total of 5 layers, finishing with the whipped cream on top. Cover with plastic wrap and refrigerate for at least 4 hours and up to overnight.

4   Run a small spatula around the edge of the cake to release it, unhook the springform pan, and transfer the cake, on the springform base, to a serving plate. Drizzle the cake with the chocolate syrup, sprinkle with the peanuts, and top with the reserved strawberries and bananas and a maraschino cherry, if desired.

MAPLE GINGERSNAP ICEBOX CAKE Substitute thin gingersnap cookies for the chocolate wafers and sweeten the whipped cream with 2 tablespoons maple syrup. Instead of fruit, sprinkle ½ cup toffee bits in between the layers for added texture and flavor.

PIE FILLING

4 Gala apples, peeled

4 McIntosh apples, peeled

1 tablespoon fresh lemon juice

2 tablespoons unsalted butter

½ cup granulated sugar

¼ cup packed light brown sugar

5 tablespoons all-purpose flour, plus more for dusting

1½ teaspoons ground cinnamon

½ teaspoon freshly grated nutmeg

¼ teaspoon ground allspice

1 teaspoon kosher salt

1 large egg, beaten

4 In a large skillet set over medium-high heat, melt the butter. Add the apples, toss to coat in the butter, and cook until softened, 5 to 7 minutes. Sprinkle both of the sugars, the flour, cinnamon, nutmeg, allspice, and salt over the apples and toss to coat evenly. Remove the pan from the heat and let cool completely.

5 On a floured surface, roll out one of the dough discs until it is ¼ inch thick. Transfer it to a 9-inch pie plate, leaving a ½-inch overhang. Prick the crust using a fork, and fill the crust with the apple mixture.

6 Roll out the second dough disc slightly thinner than ¼ inch thick. Transfer it to the top of the pie and trim the edges to about a ½-inch overhang. Pinch the top crust to the bottom and fold the overhang in, fluting the edge, or press to seal with the tines of a fork. Vent the pie by cutting 4 slits in the top, then brush with the beaten egg.

7 Transfer the pie to a baking sheet and bake until the crust is golden brown and the filling is bubbling, 45 to 50 minutes. Let cool for 20 minutes before serving. (Store in an airtight container at room temperature for up to 2 days or in the refrigerator for up to 4 days.)

bench scraper

A bench scraper may seem like a small and insignificant tool to classify as an essential, but I couldn't function in my kitchen without it. Its technical use is for baking, but it's also great for cutting and measuring bread or cookie doughs and scooping up and transferring big piles of vegetables into a skillet. This tool becomes an extension of your hand, which makes working quickly and cleanly even easier.

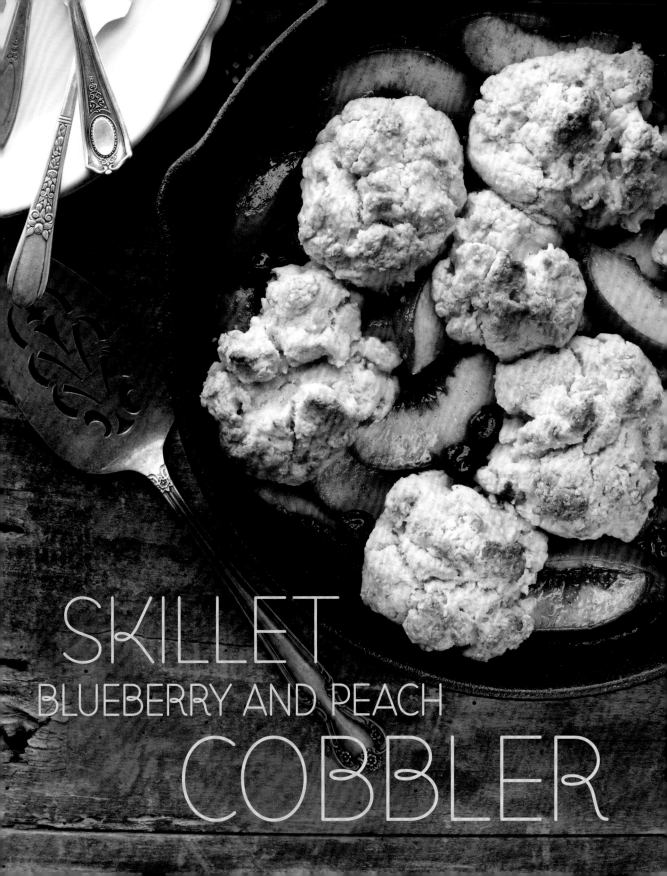

SKILLET
BLUEBERRY AND PEACH
COBBLER

FRUIT

½ cup sugar

1 tablespoon cornstarch

½ teaspoon ground cinnamon

½ teaspoon kosher salt

3 large peaches, peeled (see page 84), pitted, and cut into ½-inch-thick wedges

2½ cups blueberries

¼ teaspoon grated lemon zest (optional)

1 tablespoon fresh lemon juice

BISCUITS

1½ cups all-purpose flour

1½ tablespoons sugar

2 teaspoons baking powder

½ teaspoon baking soda

¾ teaspoons kosher salt

6 tablespoons (¾ stick) cold unsalted butter, cut into small pieces or grated

½ cup buttermilk

It's no secret that I'm in love with my cast-iron skillet. It's a topic of conversation that comes up surprisingly often and always ends with me making sure whomever I'm chatting with has one. I use it for everything from searing fish to baking dessert, and as a result I usually store it on my stovetop ready to be used at a moment's notice. I particularly love the rustic look of this dessert served in a cast-iron skillet. The fact that it can be assembled, baked, and served in the same pan makes this right up my alley. I also like to use this technique and swap in seasonal fruits. Served alongside ice cream, this warm cobbler makes for a true home-style dessert.

1 Preheat the oven to 400°F.

2 **For the fruit:** In a large bowl, combine the sugar, cornstarch, cinnamon, and salt. Add the peaches and blueberries and stir, coating the fruit evenly with the sugar mixture. Add the lemon zest (if using) and lemon juice.

3 Put the fruit filling into a cast-iron skillet and bake until fruit begins to soften and become syrupy, 15 to 20 minutes. Increase the oven temperature to 425°F.

4 **For the biscuits:** Meanwhile, in a large bowl, whisk together the flour, sugar, baking powder, baking soda, and salt. Using a food processor, a pastry cutter, or your fingertips, cut in the cold butter until the mixture resembles a coarse meal. Add the buttermilk and stir until just moistened.

5 Carefully remove the skillet from the oven. Drop 6 to 8 mounds of biscuit dough on top of the fruit. Bake until the biscuits are golden brown on top and the fruit is bubbling, about 30 minutes. Let cool for 15 minutes before serving.

CONCORD GRAPE GRANITA

WITH LIME AND MINT

¼ cup sugar

2 cups Concord grape juice

Grated zest of 1 lime

¼ cup fresh lime juice (from 2 to 3 limes)

4 sprigs fresh mint

Fleur de sel, for garnish

SERVES **4 to 6** • PREP **20 minutes plus freezing time**

Concord grape juice always makes me think of my grandma Charlotte, who served it at our family dinners on Sundays; she canned her own grape juice in season so that we could enjoy it all year long. Concord grapes are so sweet and juicy that they seem to explode in your mouth. Using the juice to make an icy granita is one of my favorite ways to enjoy this superfood. The addition of lime provides a nice tart flavor to balance out some of the sweetness. The fresh mint infused into the syrup and the sprinkle of salt gives it a bit of finesse and makes this light dessert even more refreshing. This is a perfect recipe for splurging on a high-quality sea salt like fleur de sel—sprinkled over the granita just before serving, it will give a burst of flavor, visual appeal, and even texture.

1 In a medium saucepan set over medium-high heat, combine the sugar, ½ cup of the grape juice, the lime zest, lime juice, and mint sprigs. Bring to a simmer, stirring to dissolve the sugar, and cook for 3 minutes. Remove the pan from the heat. Let cool for about 20 minutes.

2 Remove the mint sprigs and stir in the remaining 1½ cups grape juice. Pour the mixture into a 9 × 13-inch glass baking dish. Put the dish into the freezer. Every 30 minutes, scrape the mixture with a fork to break up the ice crystals and to keep the granita light and fluffy. Continue scraping every 30 minutes for at least 2 hours until an icy slush has formed.

3 Scrape the granita into glasses, sprinkle with a little fleur de sel, and serve.

GRANDMA'S BANANA-NUT SHEET CAKE

SERVES **24 (1 sheet cake)** • PREP **15 minutes** • COOK **30 minutes**

BANANA CAKE

1 cup (2 sticks) unsalted butter, at room temperature

2 cups sugar

4 large eggs, at room temperature

2 teaspoons fresh lemon juice

2 ripe medium bananas, mashed

1 cup whole milk

3 cups all-purpose flour

1 teaspoon baking soda

1 teaspoon kosher salt

This recipe defines "family recipe" to me. It came from my great-grandma Thelma and has been made on a regular basis by members of my family for more than thirty years. It's an old-fashioned foolproof cake recipe prepared in a sheet pan to feed as many as possible. But be warned if you plan to serve a crowd: At times we've had to hide this cake after baking as it tends to be addictive—one slice is never enough! The banana icing on top is every bit as good as the cake underneath and you can use it for topping cookies and other cakes as well. Fully ripe bananas are essential to this recipe. If necessary, toss your bananas into a brown paper bag overnight to speed up the process.

1 **For the banana cake:** Preheat the oven to 350°F. Butter and flour a 10.5 × 15.5-inch jelly-roll pan.

2 Using an electric mixer, cream together the butter and sugar on medium speed, until pale yellow and fluffy, about 3 minutes. Mix in the eggs, one at a time, followed by the lemon juice, mashed bananas, and milk.

3 In a separate bowl, whisk together the flour, baking soda, and salt. Slowly beat the flour mixture into the banana mixture, then beat on medium speed for 2 minutes. Spread the batter evenly in the prepared pan.

4 Bake until a cake tester inserted into the cake comes out clean, 25 to 30 minutes. Let cool.

¼ cup (½ stick)
unsalted butter, at room
temperature

1 ripe medium banana,
mashed

2 teaspoons vanilla
extract

4 cups powdered sugar

½ teaspoon kosher salt

1 cup chopped toasted
walnuts (see page 203)

5 **For the icing:** Using an electric mixer, combine the
butter, banana, vanilla, powdered sugar, and salt and
beat until smooth. If the frosting is too thick, add a
teaspoon or two of milk.

6 Frost the cake with the icing (see page 219 for details)
and sprinkle the top with the walnuts. (Store the cake,
covered tightly with plastic wrap, at room temperature for
up to 2 days.)

hand-held mixer

Unless you are a serious baker, most often
a hand-held mixer will get the job done for
all of your mixing and whisking needs, and
it takes up significantly less space in your
kitchen than a stand mixer. I own both and
find that I reach for my hand mixer a lot
more often than I use my stand mixer. It's
perfect for making a
quick batch of cookies,
whipping fresh cream,
or whisking up
some egg whites
for a soufflé or
meringues.

ESSENTIAL YELLOW BIRTHDAY CAKE
WITH VANILLA BUTTERCREAM FROSTING

SERVES 8 (one 9-inch layer cake) • **PREP 15 minutes plus freezing time** • **COOK 40 minutes**

WITH VARIATIONS

CAKE

3½ cups all-purpose flour

2 tablespoons cornstarch

2 teaspoons baking powder

1½ teaspoons baking soda

1¼ teaspoons kosher salt

1 cup (2 sticks) unsalted butter, at room temperature

2 cups sugar

4 large eggs, at room temperature

2 cups buttermilk

1 tablespoon vanilla extract

Nothing says "I love you" more than a homemade birthday cake. I'm not one to knock a boxed cake mix and definitely feel that there is a time and place for them, but if there is ever an excuse to make a really good layer cake from scratch, this is the occasion. This vanilla frosting over vanilla cake combination is crazy delicious and always works. The beautiful fluffy yellow cake has a crumbly texture and the vanilla buttercream is just sweet enough—and easily adapted to other flavorings (see variations). Here's a tip for a smooth frosting with no crumbs: Use the freezer. Wrap each layer of cake in plastic wrap and freeze overnight to make it easier to frost. For the final touch, I'm of the opinion that every homemade birthday cake deserves rainbow sprinkles.

1 **For the cake:** Preheat the oven to 350°F. Generously butter and flour two 9-inch round cake pans, line with parchment paper circles, and butter the parchment.

2 In a medium bowl, sift together the flour, cornstarch, baking powder, baking soda, and salt.

3 Using an electric mixer, cream together the butter and sugar on medium-high speed until pale yellow and fluffy, 3 to 5 minutes. Add the eggs, one at a time, beating well after each addition and scraping down the sides of the bowl. Reduce the mixer speed to low, add the buttermilk and vanilla, and mix until just combined. Slowly add the flour mixture and mix until just combined.

4 Divide the batter evenly between the prepared cake pans and tap the pans on the counter several times to get rid of any air bubbles.

continued

VANILLA BUTTERCREAM

2 cups (4 sticks) unsalted butter, at room temperature

6 cups powdered sugar

2 teaspoons kosher salt

2 teaspoons vanilla extract

¼ cup milk

½ cup rainbow sprinkles

5 Bake until golden and a cake tester inserted in the center of a cake comes out clean, 35 to 40 minutes.

6 Transfer the pans to a wire rack and let cool for 10 to 15 minutes. Run the blade of a butter knife around the edges of the pans to release the cakes. Invert the cakes onto a wire rack and discard the parchment. Let cool completely, about 1 hour. Wrap both layers in plastic wrap and freeze for at least 30 minutes or up to overnight.

7 **For the buttercream:** Using an electric mixer, beat together the butter, powdered sugar, and salt on low speed until combined, about 2 minutes. Scrape down the sides of the bowl, increase the mixer speed to medium-high, and beat until fluffy, about 3 minutes. Add the vanilla and milk and beat on medium-high speed until the frosting is light and fluffy, 3 to 5 minutes.

8 Remove the frozen cake layers from the freezer and unwrap. Put one layer on a cake stand and spread about one-third of the frosting onto the top of the layer. Put the second layer on top of the first and top with another one-third of the frosting. Spread the last one-third of the frosting on the sides. Decorate with the sprinkles and serve.

CHOCOLATE BUTTERCREAM Sift 1 cup cocoa powder together with the powdered sugar before creaming with the butter and salt.

ORANGE BUTTERCREAM Add 1 tablespoon grated orange zest to the mixture.

ALMOND BUTTERCREAM Substitute 1½ teaspoons almond extract for the vanilla extract.

FROSTING

Beautifully topped cakes, cupcakes, or cookies will have everyone fooled that your dessert was frosted at the best bakery in town. Here are a few techniques that I always rely on:

CHILL EVERYTHING. Before frosting, make sure your cake or cupcakes are completely cool. I like to put them in the freezer to get them super chilled. Also, if you are frosting a cake, apply a thin, preliminary layer of frosting, called a crumb coat, on the chilled surface and chill it again. This locks in all of the crumbs, giving you a smooth surface—this makes it much easier to apply a smooth final coat of frosting.

INVEST IN AN OFFSET SPATULA. This tool makes frosting so much easier and faster. I like having a small one on hand for things like cookies, and a larger one for frosting layer cakes.

USE ENOUGH FROSTING. The spatula should never touch the surface of the baked good; it should only be making contact with the frosting. I use the tip of the spatula with light pressure and back-and-forth strokes. Avoid lifting the spatula straight up as that could pull off crumbs.

FINISH SMOOTHLY. To give your baked goods a smooth and shiny finish, dip your spatula into hot water and dry it. Then carefully slide the heated surface over the frosting, melting it just enough to give it a smooth finish. Repeat as needed.

THANKS

This cookbook was a labor of love in the best way possible. I felt unconditional support and encouragement from so many people throughout this process, which made this challenging yet rewarding experience humbling and, most important, fun! The people who fill my kitchen day in and day out make it one of my favorite places to be. It's where the ideas and recipes on these pages were first talked about and later tested.

My family has been so instrumental in bringing this book to life. My husband, Robby, is the world's best taste tester and honest critic; with him by my side I feel that I can accomplish anything. My son, Oliver, fills my life with purpose and so much love I could burst. These recipes reflect the best of me because of my mom. She willingly tested and retested nearly every recipe in this book. Thank you to friends who felt like family throughout this process: Elinor Hutton for always pointing me in the right direction and Treva Chadwell for your incredible insight and thoughtful approach to cooking.

Thank you to my Cooking Channel and Rock Shrimp Productions (Kim Martin, Fran Alswang, and Bobby Flay) family that has helped to make my dream of *Kelsey's Essentials* a reality. To Eric Lupfer and Mark Mullett at WME for always handling the business details so that I can focus on the food. Many thanks to the team at Clarkson Potter and my editor, Rica Allannic, for believing in me.

The talents of many have made this book even more beautiful than I could have ever imagined. Sara Remington is as lovely as her photographs and Lillian Kang, Dani Fisher, and Stephanie Huntwork outdid themselves styling the elements of this book that mean so much to me.

I'm a lucky girl and never intend to take one day in the kitchen for granted.

INDEX

Note: Page references in *italics* indicate recipe photographs.